RELATIVE SPEAKING
MORE RESCUED STORIES

LYNN A JACOBSON

RELATIVE SPEAKING: MORE RESCUED STORIES

Copyright © 2022 Lynn A Jacobson. *All rights reserved.*

ISBN 978-1-66786-685-7

No part of this publication may be reproduced, distributed, or transmitted in any form or by any means, including photocopying, recording, or other electronic or mechanical methods, without the prior written permission of the author, except in the case of brief quotations embodied in critical reviews and certain other noncommercial uses permitted by copyright law.

Cover: R. Meimei Pan and Tienlyn Jacobson

DEDICATION

To my extended family—past, present, and future
I am blessed with an incredible wife, five wonderful daughters, multiple unique grandchildren, and loving in-laws and friends. Thank you for letting me into your lives and listening to my stories, which ultimately led to this book. It is for you that I dedicate these stories to keep them alive.

NOTE ON TITLE AND NAMES

It's been the guiding philosophy in our family that if we can 1) avoid smoking, 2) avoid drugs, and 3) use our adverbs correctly, we are three legs up in meeting life's challenges. A number of friends and editors of this book claim I erred when selecting my title. "It should be *Relatively Speaking*," they gently correct, "as *relative* is an adjective or noun, whereas clearly, an adverb is called for here. As an evangelist of correct adverb usage, Lynn, you should know that," they chide. No, *Relative* (the noun) was chosen on purpose. The *relative* featured in each chapter is channeling his or her own story.

Note on names: In 1958 China changed the romanization or the way words are written from the Wade-Giles system and other Anglicized words to a simplified Hanyu Pinyin system in order to make the language more accessible to the general population. The changes are inconsistent even in China, but I have noted some former spellings in parentheses as they were at the time of the stories, e.g., Beijing (Peking).

PREVIOUS BOOKS

I. Surviving Five Daughters
Family
Survival? Yes.
Recovery? Still in doubt.

II. Secrets Of A Trophy Husband
Love
Things we do for love.
Wife's favorite book.

III. Kwajalein, An Island Like No Other
Adventure
Big Bucks—Yeah!
No Taxes—Yeah!
Per Diem—Yeah!
Perfect Weather—Yeah!
Perfect Skin Diving—Yeah!
No Women—Boooo!
So Close. Almost Paradise.

IV. Rescued Stories 1
Amazing people
They claim they will write their incredible life stories—eventually.
But we know they never will—so I wrote them.

ACKNOWLEDGMENTS

The most valuable contributor to my efforts to birth this fifth book was, without doubt, Raehua Meimei Pan, my wife and lifelong companion. She's been a tough editor and critic. Every time I lost an opinion (argument) with her, I knew I would have a better product. Also contributing to my effort were two writing groups sponsored by the Avenidas Center in Palo Alto. Special thanks to Carol Pechler, my fifteen year-long supporter, and Barbara Nachman who led Avenidas memoir-writing workshops.

My youngest two daughters rescued me numerous times when I was about to be overwhelmed by the quagmire of unfamiliar writing tools and moved me to solid ground and the finish line. Working together across generations is a joy, privilege, and a gift. Thank you.

Table of Contents

Prologue i

Emma Liu Pan, Mother-in-law

1. Fleeing Terrorism—1853, Taiping Civil War, China 1
2. Fleeing Terrorism—1911, Overthrow Qing Dynasty 7
3. Little Rose 14
4. Liu Family History 23
5. Early Years 26
6. In Charge 30
7. Lots of Liu's 32
8. Where Others Fear to Tread 34
9. But Wait, There's More 38
10. A Workday Like No Other 41
11. Fleeing Shanghai 44
12. Reaching Free China 49
13. "It Was The White Dress" 51
14. The Hump 58
15. Emma Bound for America—1945 61
16. Maternal Family Tradition—Flight and Survival 66

Enlin Pan, Father-in-law

17. Pan Family History 72
18. Romantic Getaway, Sort of 77
19. Foreign Guests Only 79
20. Mr. Pan Must Report! 83
21. Together At Last 90
22. The Communists Take Over—1949 94

Allan Henry Jacobson and Charlotte Grant Jacobson, Author's Parents

23. THEM ... 104
24. How THEY Met ... 108
25. Adoption ... 111
26. Cars Cars, Cars, and More Cars ... 115
27. The Rookie ... 118
28. Flip Side of the Coin ... 121
29. Once-a-Generation Opportunity ... 123
30. That Beautiful Buick ... 127
31. FOR SALE: 1940 FORD COUPE ... 132
32. Where's Your Father, Sonny? ... 134
33. Car Buyers Have Long Memories ... 136
34. Mr. Anderson ... 138
35. Borrowed Expertise ... 141
36. Observing The Master ... 143
37. Oops, Something Awry—early 1950s ... 147
38. Creative Solutions ... 150
39. Boundaries—It's a Guy Thing ... 152
40. A Penny For Your Thoughts ... 157
41. Aunt Bea ... 159

The Phenomenal Mr. H. M. Lui, Uncle-in-law

42. Your Parents Would Never Forgive Me… ... 165
43. The Pan/Lui Connection ... 170
44. Auntie Lui ... 174
45. Swimming to a New Life ... 177
46. The Almost Robbery ... 180
47. We Must Have Lunch ... 184
48. No Words Needed ... 189
49. Head Housekeeper ... 191
50. Gardener ... 194
51. Wait! There's More…Shorts ... 197

Photos

1. 1947 Emma's Father (Liu Yi Xian) visiting Parents' Tomb, Hangzhou ... 20
2. 1936 Emma's parents (Liu Yu Ning Xian & Liu Yi Xian) Winter in Hangzhou home after mother's illness ... 21
3. 1917 Baby Emma and Nurse ... 22
4. 1936 Emma on West Lake, Hangzhou ... 22
5. 1936 Emma, College Student ... 29
6. 1942 Enlin and Emma Together at Last in Chungking ... 48
7. 1943 Emma's International Grad School Exam Pass ... 57
8. 1944 Emma's Ship Pass to California ... 60
9. 1945 Emma Expecting First Child ... 64
10. 1946 Emma—New York Style ... 65
11. 1943 Enlin in Chongqing (Chungking) ... 69
12. 1943 Emma Takes a Ride ... 70
13. 1945 Enlin—International Businessman ... 71
14. 1932 Enlin's Mother (Soong Tsu Tsen) ... 76
15. 1942 Enlin's Father (Pan Shi-Chao) ... 76
16. 1944 Enlin Pan on Newsweek Cover ... 86
17. 1945 San Francisco Chronicle Announcement Feb. 11, 1945 ... 87
18. 1945 Emma and Enlin Wedding Picture ... 88
19. 1945 Emma and Enlin at Niagara Falls ... 89
20. 1971 Enlin at 66 After Heart Attack ... 100
21. 1904 The Three Orphaned Grant Sisters: Author's mother, Charlotte Jacobson (on left), Margo Black, and Nell West ... 102
22. 1950 Allan Showing Off his 33' Owens Cabin Cruiser St. Albans Bay, Lake Minnetonka ... 103
23. 1963 Catch of the Day (Allan Jacobson squatting on left) Pompano Beach, Florida ... 103
24. 1947 Allan & Charlotte Jacobson taking a dip in Lake Minnetonka (St. Albans Bay) in front of our Minnesota home ... 110
25. Mr. H. M. Lui, Uncle-in-law ... 164
26. 1972 Luis and Pans at Luis's Daughter's Wedding ... 164
27. 1988 The Future: Emma & Her Six Grandchildren ... 203

PROLOGUE

Everybody loves a good story. Individual tastes vary but the draw of a good story is undeniable. Even the standard greetings: "What's up?" "How's it going?" or "Where ya been?" often elicit, "Do you have a good story?" New jokes have the potential of being good stories, albeit of a short variety and, according to my daughters, mine often inflict pain rather than elicit laughs.

Every Saturday when I lived on Kwajalein (a small tropical island, part of the Marshall Islands, Pacific) in the early 1970s, our scuba club sponsored a dive boat to remote, uninhabited islands halfway up the atoll, ten to thirty miles from our main island. Typically thirty club members would enjoy a day of recreational diving in untouched waters—taking photos, searching for gorgeous cowrie shells, or just enjoying the thousands of fish in their natural tropical habitat checking us out as well. Once anchored, novice divers would hit the water and immediately scatter a few hundred yards in all directions to scour the virgin hunting grounds.

The dive master in charge would patiently wait until only the two assigned safety divers remained aboard, don his mask, flop backward into the water, sink straight down the twenty to thirty feet to the bottom and, as often as not, have better luck right under the boat than those who searched further afield. Experienced divers know that treasures of the sea can be found right under one's nose (or boat in this case), if one just takes the time to look.

Fine. What does this have to do with finding good stories? There is a treasure trove of amazing stories right under our very noses that we overlook every day. It's the unassuming elders among us—the ones ensconced in the corner during a social gathering who appear more like permanent fixtures than guests. They lost the incentive to tell **their** stories years ago when we were all too busy to listen. As a result, they no longer reminisced about the *old days*. The adit to their trove of good stories had been sealed for years, but there's still paydirt to be found. The storyteller's task is to pry open the entrances and mine the contents. We just need to ask the right questions.

The stories I find most valuable come from these elders (particularly grandparents) who still retain oral historic details of their early experiences—fresh enough to lend credence to their telling. My interpretation of these stories is spliced together by collecting tidbits here and there from my sources over time, rather than gathering all the details of a story in one take. I filled in gaps in the stories of these extraordinary personalities as best I could while trying to stay faithful to what made them tick and the standards of the times. I hope to do my elders justice in telling their stories.

Lynn A Jacobson
(Name at birth: Lynn Melroy Hopland)

EMMA LIU PAN,
MOTHER-IN-LAW

1.
FLEEING TERRORISM

—

1853, TAIPING CIVIL WAR, CHINA

It was early in the Taiping Civil War (1850-1864 rebellion), perhaps one of the deadliest military conflicts in history, accounting for over twenty million deaths. The undisciplined soldiers on both sides, the Han Hakka Taiping Heavenly Kingdom and the Manchu-led Qing dynasty, were guilty of plundering, killing, raping, and burning alike.

Fire had been raging all night throughout the city accompanied by a horrible nonstop cacophony of shrieks, cries, and shouts—indescribable suffering. The young woman was terror-stricken listening to what was happening outside their tightly sealed compound. Her husband had stepped out to assess the situation a few days before and had not yet returned. Servants, huddled together, sobbed in despair and fear, contemplating their inevitable fate.

Suddenly a piercing cry rang out from the frightened group—FIRE! A flying ember from somewhere nearby had found its target and set their wooden compound ablaze.

"Go, go quickly. Run, run! Save yourselves!" the young mistress shouted to her servants.

"Oh, Taitai (mistress). Even dogs protect their masters. How could we possibly leave our young mistress in such a dire situation as this? No, we must stay to protect you!"

"And what about the little one?" added the nurse as she clutched the child to her breast (referring to the young mistress's three-year old daughter.) The nurse, with eyes bulging, lips quivering, and frozen with fear, was half-mad thinking about the plight of the little one.

"No more talk. Run. I command you all to run, run for your lives!"

With that, she dashed into her bedroom chambers. Quickly, she covered both arms under her sleeves with numerous gold bracelets, stuffed handfuls of her more valuable jewelry into her pockets, grabbed several long silk scarves out of her bureau, and finally slipped a pair of scissors into her pocket as she bolted from the room.

She pulled her daughter from the nurse's arms and secured her to her back with two scarves. As she left the house, she glanced back one last time and screamed in a choked voice, "Run for your lives. May Buddha protect each of you. We may meet again in our next life."

Finally, the heat of the fire drove the last of the household from the house—they fled in all directions. Life, as they had known it, was over.

The young woman ran as fast as she dared in the direction of the city gate while taking every precaution to avoid discovery. Any suspicious sound instantly drove her to seek cover. Corpses lay everywhere in grotesque and gruesome states along her path. The horrific sight, thick eye-burning smoke, acrid smell, and blood-bathed landscape—all made her violently ill. Time and again, she had to hide in the shadows while panicked citizens rushed past searching for refuge—any place to hide. Marauders on both sides of the war were looting with abandonment.

Once, when she heard frantic steps approaching from behind, she squeezed herself and her child down under some wooden planks—just in time. A man and a woman were being pursued by a half dozen laughing soldiers brandishing long knives— almost as if it were a game. She heard a swishing sound, saw the silvery flash of a steel blade followed by a gushing of blood from the headless man as he collapsed to the ground. The head, eyes still open, rolled down the street.

Two of the soldiers caught up with his hysterically shrieking wife. They celebrated their success by shouting to each other, grabbing her arms, and dragging her along with them. The other soldiers busied themselves over the headless body searching his pockets and the small bundle he had been carrying—the spoils of war. The scene was not far from where the young mother and her child hid, watching in disbelief. Were it not for the soldiers concentrating on divvying up their share of the loot, she would undoubtedly have been discovered.

She thought of the fateful disappearance of her husband. It was all too much, and she passed out. She didn't know whether she was out for a few minutes or an hour, but when she awoke, the soldiers were gone and the headless man was spread before her with dogs sniffing at what remained. Incredibly, the child had slept through it all. The mother's mind cleared—she knew if she wanted them to live, she had to get out of there fast. She focused, turned, and headed toward the east city gate.

She found the approach to the gate clear of both soldiers and rebels. The gate was locked as expected, so she cautiously followed the half hidden old stone pathway leading to the turrets atop the city wall—a pathway she knew from her explorations as a child. Even though she was anxious to hasten her escape, she paused long enough at the top to absorb the sight of an entire city engulfed in flames—the night sky tinted an eerie bright red—the red of hell.

The ambiance on the other side of the wall offered a sharp contrast; all was serene and quiet. There were no soldiers in sight. They probably saw no reason to man posts about to be overrun by the opposing rebel army anyway. Their time was better spent rummaging through the ashes of the city one last time to find as much loot as they could before abandoning it altogether.

She pulled out the silk scarves salvaged during her hasty escape from her burning home and tied them end-to-end to make a scarf rope several yards in length. She added extra knots between scarf ends to give her better gripping power on what was otherwise a slippery rope. Next, she fastened one end of the rope as securely as she could around the lowest turret. After carefully scanning the area immediately outside of the wall to convince herself all was clear, she dropped the free end of her silk scarf-rope over the wall. She tightened the scarf that bound her child to her back and precariously lowered them both slowly, hand over hand to the ground.

This high-class lady with bound feet who was used to having servants obey her slightest whim, was utterly exhausted. She was unaccustomed to even the slightest form of exertion. The weight of the gold bracelets on her arms plus the child on her back grew even heavier now as the fading adrenaline rush of the day's intense events took its toll. Her face and delicate hands were bruised and bleeding from the rough surface of the stone wall. She only dared to rest on the ground for a minute while she untied the child, and with her face close to her daughter's ear whispered: "Good baby, Muma loves you. Let's walk. Hush, hush baby. I'm right here—not a sound."

They had covered only a few hundred yards through the brush, when the child began to whimper. She was tired, hungry, and ached from being restrained so long. The mother cautioned: "Shh, shh, baby, don't cry. The long-haired bandits will come." She picked up the child, carried her in her arms, and pushed on.

Some farm buildings came into sight. She put the child down to let her walk a bit and to rest her own back. The two of them followed a small path that skirted the buildings. The child started to cry once again. This time she would not be soothed. Men's voices were heard somewhere. The mother assessed the situation, darted quickly into the thick bushes in the field and disappeared, leaving the child on the path alone. Abandoned, the child howled even more loudly.

Several men came noisily down the trail from the direction of the farmhouse towards the howling child. They were bearded with long hair and wore red waist bands, which secured their mostly black tattered clothing. Some were armed with knives, some with spears.

"There. Look over there. Here's a little girl for us. Baby, baby, where is your Mama?"

The little girl cried louder. The men and their rough voices frightened her. There was a cruel torturous pastime among the rebels, people were told. They would seize little children, dip their hair in oil as wicks to burn, and push the heads of spears through their bowels, holding their little bodies up as live candles. One of the men in this group suggested they have some fun with this child.

"Come, come, let's burn a candle," he laughed.

The young mother in hiding wanted to dash out to save her child. She knew it would be suicide for both. But she had her scissors ready. She would die by her own hand. She could never allow herself or her child to be molested or abused in any way.

A strong and commanding voice rang out: "I forbid anyone to do such a thing. Haven't you killed enough already?"

This man picked up the child in his strong arms, and said: "Little one, wherever your Papa and Mama are, they will probably come for you. Don't cry. Don't get yourself killed." He carried the child towards an outhouse and put her down just inside the door, saying: "You, little one, stay here. Your mama will come for you soon enough."

He rejoined his men on the path and said loudly: "I left the little girl inside the outhouse." He knew that somewhere nearby, a desperate parent or parents were listening. Then the men left together and headed towards the burning city.

The young woman and her daughter identified in this story were the great grandmother and grandmother of Emma Pan, the author's mother-in-law. Emma's writings include historic accounts of women in her family who like her, had been forced to flee military hostilities and terrorism. Her writings were based on oral history repeated many times by her mother to her and her sisters when they were very young, about her great-grandmother, her grandmother, and her own mother. The following few chapters are her stories.

2.

FLEEING TERRORISM

–

1911, OVERTHROW QING DYNASTY

Sixty plus years passed since the little three-year-old girl and her mother narrowly escaped certain death in their flight from the Taiping Rebellion. The little one had grown up to be a beautiful woman and married well. But now she was old and widowed and had come to live with her only married daughter (Emma's mother) in Hangzhou, a city renowned for its beautiful West Lake and its beautiful women.

Shortly after Emma's grandmother's arrival in early 1911, the latest revolution (October 1911-February 1912) was in full force. The Qing dynasty was about to be overthrown after 276 years of Manchu rule over China. Her own daughter (Emma's mother) had just given birth to a boy, her third child and third son. The old lady had become very ill at the same time, and her end was expected any day. No doctor could be found to assist the family because of the revolution. The young mother was overtaxed, caring for both her dying mother and her newborn—and enduring anxiety over the safety of the rest of her family, that her breast milk had dried up. The household servants searched everywhere but could not locate a badly needed wet nurse for the baby; they had to improvise and fed the baby thin rice soup and very soft rice paste.

One morning when she was trying to feed the baby some soft paste, a servant attending the sick grandmother rushed down the stairs panting and shouting: "Quick, Taitai (mistress), it is not good with Lao Taitai (the old mistress). Come quickly!" The daughter put her baby down in the middle of her own bed and ran upstairs. The old lady had just let out her last breath—she had expired. She was forever set free of the worries and sufferings of the many more wars yet to come in this troubled land.

Though the old lady's death had not been unexpected, the daughter was overcome by grief. She knelt by the bed, holding her mother's stiffening hand tenderly, buried her face in its palm, and cried silently.

The servants lit two white candles and placed them at the foot of the bed. The dress and shroud, which had been prepared for this event, were made ready. Their elderly manservant was dispatched to have the old lady's coffin sent in just as the two older boys, ages six and seven, burst into the room and rushed to their mother. Suddenly they realized that their grandmother was dead. They stopped abruptly and froze, staring at her motionless form on the bed, her face ash-colored, though still gentle as though she were asleep.

Turning towards her sons, their mother beckoned them to come kneel. The boys moved slowly towards the bed, knelt, and kowtowed. Three times thus done, they got up quickly and cried out urgently: "Muma, the baby! He would not eat, he does not move."

With a sense of foreboding, the mother immediately turned her attention to the new emergency and rushed downstairs. A piercing cry was heard immediately. The servants followed her down to see what had happened. They found their young mistress holding the baby, frantically trying to dislodge large pieces of rice paste from his mouth with her finger. It was no use, the baby had too much rice paste stuffed deep down his tiny throat and had choked. He too was gone.

"We only wanted to feed him!" the two boys, crying beyond control, blurted out. They did not understand that they had unknowingly killed their little brother. A maid gently took the lifeless baby from his mother's arms. The young woman slowly sank down and fainted.

Two coffins, one large and one tiny, were hastily delivered. The bodies of the old and the newborn were washed, dressed, laid in the caskets, and placed in the front parlor according to custom. An offering table was set up with a white mourning cloth strung above. A photo of the grandmother was hung on the wall above the coffin. The customary 49 days of mourning began.

Everywhere in the country, one city after another declared its independence. In Hangzhou, as in many other cities, men hastened to cut off their pigtails, symbols of the 276 years of oppression imposed upon Chinese men by the Manchus. People had no safe place to go, and they were anxious for the revolution to be over. They locked the doors of their houses and shops to protect themselves from constant looting and waited. The tide turned quickly against the Qing Dynasty, and on February 12, 1912, Hsian-T'ung, the last emperor of China, abdicated.

During the last few months of the revolution, life was fraught with hardships and tribulations. It was very difficult for the isolated city residents to get any reliable information about the war's progress beyond their own neighborhood. They bore the hardships as well as they could but left their fate to Providence.

One afternoon there came a heavy banging on the front gate, with several male voices demanding, "Open up!" The only male servant, too old to be conscripted, went to check on the commotion and returned shaking with fear. In a trembling voice he informed his mistress that there was a group of soldiers at their outer gate insisting to be let in.

The young woman asked, "Are they government soldiers or Revolutionists?"

"Taitai, I do…I do not know. Either way, it is not good."

The banging grew louder and more aggressive.

"Open the door, and let them in," said the mistress.

"But Taitai, suppose they...they are soldiers?"

"They will come in anyway. Either we open the door for them, or they will break it in."

She saw there was no way out. She ordered all the women servants to the back of the kitchen with the children and bade the male servant to admit the unwanted guests. She crossed over the common family room to the front parlor and faced the big photo of her mother. "Muma, will your spirit please help and protect us from any harm and evil?"

Threatening footsteps mixed with loud, boisterous shouts emanated from across the courtyard. Then the approaching soldiers spotted the white mourning hangings across the top of the opened doors. Facing them, swathed in heavy coarse burlap mourning attire from head to toe, stood a small, slender young woman (Meimei's grandmother) in front of two coffins, one adult sized, one very small. She stood erectly; her eyes leveled straight into their captain's eyes without fear. The soldiers stopped in their tracks halfway across the courtyard. One man even spat when confronted with the unlucky sight of coffins. The mistress became bolder after her calculated gamble of meeting the intruders face-to-face had the effect she hoped for. Now she had their attention. Giving no ground, she stepped forward a few paces. With a slightly bowed head, she swept her hand towards the coffins, and said in a steady but sorrowful voice: "I must beg your forgiveness. As you can see, here lies my honorable mother and my newborn child who both passed twelve days ago. I regret not being in the position to invite you into my house. If you are short of money, I have but a few copper coins, and you may have them. If you are hungry and in need of a meal, I can offer only a few grains of coarse rice, for we've had no food for many days now. I am at a loss to offer any assistance to you. But please, will you kindly inform me how the war is going? You see, we have not left the house since the death of my poor mother and child, nor has anyone come to see us."

"Where is your husband?"

"He went to the capital for business many months ago. We have not heard from him since. Buddha have mercy, I pray he is still alive, somewhere."

The soldiers became very quiet—almost respectful. They all looked to the man who appeared to be their leader for clues as to how they should respond. The man appeared bewildered as well. He shifted his booted feet, spat on the ground, and said in a dejected voice: "Damn, we had to choose this house. Let's get out of this cursed unlucky place fast before it infects us." They turned and left without hesitation. The leader was just about to pass through the front gate as well when he paused, slowly turned, and commanded the shivering servant, "Bring me a large writing brush and ink." The surprised servant looked to his mistress for instruction. She motioned him to do as ordered. Presently, he brought out a big writing brush and an inkwell from the house. He put some water in the inkwell and made black ink. The soldier dipped the brush in the ink, raised his arm, and wrote two big characters meaning "Mourning" on the outside of the front gate's two panels. He called out to the young lady: "Woman, with these, you will most unlikely be bothered by anyone else." Whether the woman lovingly tending to her mother's and child's spirits made him recall his own family or his own benevolent gesture had kindled kindness in his heart, he left with a calmer countenance than when he arrived.

Many days passed without further incident as the man predicted. But then one morning there was again a loud banging on the front door. Again, the people in the house became frightened. The banging grew louder. Then the young woman became excited as she heard her husband's voice yelling, "Open the door, Ah Chang, it's me, your Master!"

Upon hearing his master's voice, the manservant ran quickly to open the gate. The master, his face ruggedly browned and dressed in uniform, entered accompanied by a small entourage of men. He strode briskly across the courtyard to the big parlor, took in the scene in the parlor in one glance, and asked his wife hoarsely, pointing to the little coffin: "Who is this?"

"The little baby. He lived only a few days."

"The baby?" he asked in puzzlement and pulled back. "What baby?"

"My baby, a boy," the woman looked at him quizzically as though saying, "You didn't know that we had another baby?"

"Your baby?" The man stood very rigidly, looking at his wife in mounting disbelief and apparent anger. "I left home so long ago. Whose baby is this?"

It took a full minute before the woman realized the implication of his questions. Suddenly, she drew herself up, looked up to her husband with tear-filled eyes, and angry words rolled out like a torrent, lashing at him like the thunderous beating of a drum of war.

"Good question! You left home seven months ago to make a revolution. You left your family without any protection. By Buddha's mercy, you came back in one piece to find your family still alive. You do not ask how and when my mother died. You do not ask how the family fared for themselves during these horrible months. You do not ask how I managed. You do not ask thousands of other questions a good husband should ask about his family. But you—what do you do? You suspect your wife of being unfaithful the minute you set foot into your own house. I have had enough!" Her voice rose to a high pitch, almost hysterical, with choking sobs. She turned abruptly and retreated to her bedroom.

The man was astonished by his wife's outburst. In all the turmoil, he had not noticed his two young sons standing not too far away from him with wide-open, frightened eyes fixed upon him. They said nothing and bolted from the room. He spotted an old maid near the door about to disappear as well, when he motioned for her to come near. "I am confused—tell me—what has happened in my house since I have been away?"

"Master, the old lady died about a month ago. Taitai had just given birth to your son a few days earlier, but she had no milk—the stress of the war and lack of nourishment. We could not find a wet nurse for him. He died within a few hours of the old lady. Master, we have been through very hard times…extreme danger everywhere, every day. We are lucky to be alive. It is good that you are home now."

The master bent his head and covered his face with his hands, fighting back his tears. He took a deep breath, got up and walked quickly to their bedroom. He found his wife sitting in front of the long windows, which opened onto their private walled garden. Her eyes, red from sobbing, stared vacantly into space—her hands lay on her lap endlessly twisting a wet silk handkerchief. She gave no acknowledgment of his presence as he approached her. It was then that he saw how incredibly thin she had become and realized how much she had suffered.

He came close to her and gently pleaded, "Please forgive me. I'm such a fool. These last seven months I worried about you and the children all the time. I was so happy and excited when I learned the city had been liberated, for then I could make it home to be with you all once again. I was confused and could not make sense of it; I was overtaken by all I saw, I lost my mind. Will you ever forgive me for what I said? I promise, I'll never doubt you again."

Slowly and gently, he picked up her hand and held it lovingly in both of his hands. She did not turn her head but did not withdraw her hand either. After a short pause she sighed and with a reproachful voice murmured, "Where are your manners? You need to pay respect to my mother."

3.
LITTLE ROSE

It was generally understood in the Liu family that Emma, the seventh of eight children and second of three daughters, was the most studious child (earning her the nickname of Little Intelligent One.) She engaged with Liu Yi-Xian, her scholarly father, on an intellectual level far more in depth than her siblings. She adored her father and cherished every moment they spent together. He likewise doted on her. He would lovingly prepare a fresh inkwell of Chinese black ink each school day so that upon her arrival home, she could happily practice her calligraphy at her sunlit desk.

Emma's mother, Yu Ning Xian, also took a special interest in Emma's education even though they were from two very different eras. Her mother (1876-1942) grew up with bound feet while the Empress Dowager was on the throne while Emma (1917-2011) was raised as a modern woman shortly after the establishment of the Republic.

Emma speculated several years later that perhaps her mother saw in her the salvation of women in the modern world—one without the dated codes of conduct or arbitrary restrictions that stifled their achievements. She encouraged Emma to pursue her own interests every chance she could, to apply herself diligently to her academic studies, and to explore life's lessons.

One summer at the end of sixth grade, when Emma just turned eleven, her mother took her on a long trip to Nanjing (Nanking) as a special treat to spend some time with her father. He was there on an extended business trip and not due to return to Hangzhou until early fall. This visit was the highlight of the year for Emma especially as she was the only one of her siblings invited.

One evening, as Emma's father prepared to join a group of his male business associates at a private dinner party, he was caught off guard by his wife's suggestion (a thinly veiled insistence), "You need to take Emma with you to your dinner party this evening." Then, to justify her request added, "It would be so good for her to get out of the house and spend more time with you. After all, that's why we came all this way in the first place —she needs more *father time*."

He knew that such a request (demand) would prove rather awkward for both him and his business associates and was reluctant to comply.

When Emma heard her mother's proposal, it was all she could do to contain herself. She wanted to jump up and down and shout, "Please, please, Papa, please take me with you!" but forced herself to act in a more dignified manner to prove she was worthy of accompanying her father to an adult function. Her father noted Emma's eager countenance while concluding that to resist his wife's request would be futile (if not fatal.) The domestic repercussions of not taking Emma would far outweigh the negative feedback from his associates for bringing her. Anyway, his high social standing in the group gave him considerable latitude to do whatever he wished. Off the two of them went, father and a very happy bouncy eleven-year-old who was quite unaware of what the evening events would entail.

When they arrived at the restaurant, Emma discovered about a dozen very distinguished-looking older gentlemen already assembled in the reserved private room closed off from the main dining area in a very upscale hotel. She recognized several of the men, who had been guests at their home one time or another. They were initially quite taken aback by her presence but nonetheless greeted her with courtesy. Soon everyone adjusted to the new arrangement and settled in.

In short order, a very elegantly dressed, middle-aged female attendant appeared, armed with brushes and several narrow slips of writing paper. She immediately worked her way around the large round table and, one by one, solicited requests from the dinner guests. Each man gave her a name which she wrote down on a separate slip. The long narrow slip of paper with both the patron and a girl's name was called "Jiao-Tiao-Tze" or "Courtesan Calling Slip".

Emma thought excitedly, *those names don't sound like normal food dishes. They must be ordering some very exotic foreign dishes I've never heard of before. How wonderful!* Listening more intently, she thought she heard "Lily" and "Violet" mentioned. *Those don't sound like food. Oh my goodness, they sound like flowers. They're ordering flowers! Flowers for dinner? I've never had that before—must be some exotic adult dishes.*

When the attendant reached Emma's seat, she smiled at her, but addressed her father, "And whom would our young Miss wish to be with?" Emma was at a total loss. *I'm with my father,* she thought. *I don't need to be with anyone else. What does she mean, 'be with?' Can't she see, I'm a big girl. I don't need a babysitter.*

Rather than protest, Emma made the wise decision to wait and see where this would all lead. It was all so new to her, and she didn't want to do anything that might embarrass herself or her father. More than anything else she wanted to prove to him that bringing her along was the right decision.

After a brief discussion, her father asked, "Whom would you recommend?" They finally concluded Little Rose would probably be the best fit. This discussion only intensified Emma's puzzlement. *Little Rose? What do they mean? What's going on?* She was beginning to realize that this world was completely unfamiliar to her. Confused, she pulled back further. She could only wait to see what happened next.

Shortly after the food and second round of wine were served, several young ladies, each accompanied by an instrument-toting musician, burst en masse through the double door entrance and flooded the room unannounced. Several of the ladies recognized their usual patrons and sat behind them accordingly with their personal musicians taking up their own stations further back. The remaining ladies found their assignees by referring to the slips given to them by the attendant and coquettishly inquired, "Mr. So and So?" Emma was transfixed and barely made a move—she just tried to take it all in, with no idea what would happen next, and subtly inched closer to her father for reassurance.

Finally, a single girl, perhaps only a year older than Emma herself, was left standing in the middle of the room, confused. She examined her slip several times and hesitantly inquired, "Is young Mr. Liu here?" Everyone laughed which made the shy girl all the more self-conscious and disorientated until one of the men, seeing her plight, took pity on her, smiled, and pointed to Emma. The young hostess, wishing to avoid further embarrassment, moved swiftly out of the spotlight and positioned herself next to and slightly behind Emma. They both froze knowing neither what to say nor what to do. Neither had experienced such an awkward situation before. They stared at each other for several seconds; then spontaneously, realizing how incongruous it all was, broke into serious cases of preteen giggles.

The girls suddenly noticed all other activity in the room had ceased; all eyes of the diners and sing-song girls alike were upon them. The girls stared back. Then as if someone hit the reset button, they started to giggle all over again. The party picked up right where it had left off and from then on, everyone ignored the two of them as if this were a normal occurrence for a typical evening dinner party.

Emma had read enough books and gleaned enough tidbits from older children to know these 'sing-song' girls were from a brothel, but she had never met one before, had no idea what they looked like nor how they acted compared to ordinary girls.

Seeing her plight, her father attempted to reduce Emma's confusion by giving her a brief, heavily watered-down explanation as to what these women's functions were at such events:

"These ladies are here to entertain the diners during their meals. Each in turn will sing, accompanied by her own musician, to entertain her assigned dinner guest for the evening. They are to be gracious and charming to their patrons and make them feel attended to and important—in other words, they're here to sweep away their patrons' worries and make them happy for the few hours they are here. Sometimes a patron will join in the singing, sometimes not—their choice."

Her father did not go into further detail, but Emma could guess the nature of her father's omissions, particularly activities that might occur in private later in the evening. At eleven years of age however, she was short on details. This was, after all, still a time of concubines (who were not officially banned until 1949) and rich idle men.

Emma was keenly aware that her father was being entertained by his own sing-song girl like the other dinner guests but he seemed more formal (i.e., well behaved) and treated her with considerable courtesy. Their conversation seemed more subdued than the other more boisterous couples in the room.

Emma and Little Rose talked quietly but incessantly for the rest of the evening, oblivious of other goings-on. Each wanted to know all about the life of the other. Each knew this was a rare opportunity to learn about the *other side*—the *what-if* side. Emma learned that after her father died, Little Rose had been sold into the brothel from the countryside by her uncle. Her family was too poor to even feed her. She told Emma that the most difficult part of all was how she missed her mother so terribly.

"I'm a novice—I'm in-training to learn the trade. It will be a few years yet before I will earn my place as a full-fledged, fully trained 'sing-song girl.'" Emma asked, "Have you ever wanted to run away and maybe go to school?" The girl sighed, "No, this is my lot. I've accepted that. My only hope is that I meet a nice man who will buy me out of the brothel and treat me well."

Their conversation migrated to the "Divine Scheme" that played upon mortals and how Emma was born into a well-to-do family while her companion was born into less fortuitous circumstances. They were incredibly open and frank with each other in their discourse—why not? There was no downside—no risk to their conversation. They asked, they answered, they listened and laughed, they taught each other about worlds they could normally only imagine. Many of their questions were so frank, they surprised even themselves, questions they wouldn't even dare ask their closest friends.

After a couple hours of intense conversation where they seldom lost eye contact, Emma felt so moved that she touched her companion's hand. Little Rose smiled and responded, "I would like to sing you a song. I'm supposed to do that anyway, but this song is special, and I sing it only for you." Her voice was so young and brought such freshness to her song that Emma was transfixed; a tear came to her eye—no, several tears. She couldn't decide whether she should laugh or cry—both at once if she could. She had never before been so moved. When they parted, both felt enriched from the experience of having met the other, but sad as well, knowing full well they would never meet again. *In another time and another world, we would have been best friends*, Emma thought as she and her father departed. Looking back through the door that closed behind them, she saw Little Rose staring at her, sitting erect with unashamed tears streaming down her face. A best friend found—a best friend lost. All in one evening.

They were the first to leave, before the remaining diners surrendered to the effects of too-much drink and before the evening's activities swung further into the adult end of the party spectrum. Father and daughter rode home in silence until her father, seeing Emma in such deep thought, gently asked her a single question, "Are you glad you accompanied me tonight?"

"Oh yes," came the immediate reply as she straightened up and tried to smile—perhaps to appear more adultlike. Perhaps she was more adultlike.

"Well, how did it go?" asked her mother. Emma answered, "Fine. And oh, I met a girl, and she sang to me. I'm tired now and wish to go to bed." Once she reached her room, she pondered, *I wonder if my father will ever be invited to his men's group dinner again.* Then she laughed to herself, *I'm sure I'll not be welcomed back. I hope Little Rose will be alright. I never had a best friend before…* was her last thought before falling asleep.

The memory of that night's dinner party in Nanjing with her father, his friends, and Little Rose stuck with Emma forever and had a lasting effect. She could not stop thinking of Little Rose. The contrast between their two lives that particular evening heavily influenced her pursuit of women's advocacy and child welfare as her chosen life's work.

Emma and her father never spoke of that evening again.

1947
Emma's Father (Liu Yi Xian) visiting Parents' Tomb, Hangzhou

1936
Emma's parents (Liu Yu Ning Xian & Liu Yi Xian)
Winter in Hangzhou home after mother's illness

1917
Baby Emma and Nurse

1936
Emma on West Lake, Hangzhou

4.
LIU FAMILY HISTORY

Emma's father and mother were Liu Yi Xin and Yu Ning Xian. Their parents were cousins and both Hunan Ningxiang people; both of their fathers were high-ranking officials in the Qing Dynasty. At one time, Yi Xin's father (Emma's grandfather) was simultaneously governor of both Jiangsu and Zhejiang provinces.

    Following his father's death, Yi Xin lived alone with his mother. The tribal people in this region bullied orphans and widows to the point of murder in order to steal their possessions. When Yi Xin learned that he and his mother were subjects of such a plot, he escaped in the middle of the night carrying her on his back. He soon joined the revolutionary movement led by Sun Yat-Sen. When the new national government was established, he rose to the powerful position of senior general in the Revolutionary Army in charge of the treasury. Yi Xin, a straight-forward Hunanese, often talked about his fellow senior officers, Huan Xing and Chiang-Kai-shek whom he greatly distrusted.

    Yi Xin and Ning Xian's marriage had been pre arranged by their parents so Yi Xin was not allowed to marry the younger sister whom he truly loved. The sister who was wise, virtuous, and loved reading, never married. The couple did not enjoy a harmonious marriage—their personalities were too different. In her early years, Ning Xian was a typical "Tai siu jia" (eldest daughter from a privileged family who loved to dress up and party) in contrast to Yi Xin who was a down-to-earth and proper Buddhist.

Several years later, in an attempt to influence Yi Xin through Ning Xian, Chiang-Kai-shek offered to match his second son with Yi Xin's daughter, Emma (Tsenho), but she turned him down.

Emma's parents had eight children, five boys and three girls (the third youngest died a few days following his birth). Yi Xin was a very strict patriarch. His children had to rise at dawn each day to practice calligraphy. As an incentive he placed three coppers (coins) in the ink stone which would be claimed by the first child to get up and begin their studies. He also instructed their tutor to include biographies, and the classics such as the Analects of Confucius in their studies.

At home, Yi Xin taught the children to respect the elders, filial piety, courteousness and humility, fraternity between brothers and sisters, and kindness to all, including servants. Elders must be seated at dinner first. Children must not interrupt adults. He applied Confucian teachings to raising their children. Anyone who didn't comply with house rules would be severely chastised and punished. The children were scared of their father, and no one dared disobey the house rules.

Yi Xin had the strong and upright, rather-die-than-surrender military type of character. At that time there was widespread poverty, and he became disillusioned with the Nationalist government. He published a strong anti-Chiang Kai Shek speech, gave up his high-ranking official position, his rich life and social position. He even left his family, retreating to Hengshan, Hunan and joined a Taoist sect to lead a contemplative life, doing good works for the locals.

Nonetheless Yi Xin missed his family and returned in 1947 to Hangzhou to visit them. He had a long white beard and flowing robe, and became a kind and forgiving old man. His life was very frugal and selfless, and he often said, "I am building blessings for my family." He often gave money or literally the clothes off his back to beggars on the street. On his return a year later to Nanyue in Hengshan, he gave away his entire savings of two silver coins.

Yi Xin passed away in 1949, the year of the official Communist takeover. The family received a letter written shortly before he died in which he said he was very sick and had no money left. Many years later, Emma, my wife's mother, sent his grandson Yao Li to search for his grave on Nanyue Mountain. Yao Li showed his grandfather's photo and one of the lady monks recognized Yi Xin as her grandfather's lifetime friend at the Ban Shan Monastery, and they were able to locate the grave which had been tended all those years. Emma sent money to rebuild the tomb. In 2012 Meimei, her brother and his family flew to Changsha and took cabs, a train to Guangzhou, and a van up Hengshan mountain. There they stayed in freezing rooms and trekked with local people, one his old friend's widow, to his rebuilt gravesite, where they were finally able to make offerings, set off firecrackers, and perform a kowtow ceremony. They learned how their grandfather had used his money and time to help local people, and while missing his family, as a philosopher hermit, had lived out his days according to his principles.

5.
EARLY YEARS

Neither my wife's mother, Emma Liu, nor her father, Enlin Pan, pursued their life paths in straight lines.

At one time, my wife, Meimei's father, Enlin, spent part of an academic year enrolled in an all-girls school in Hangzhou (Hangchou), whereas a dozen years later Meimei's mother spent two years at an all-boys school, also in Hangzhou. For Enlin, it was the only way he could study music, not offered at any of the boys schools. For Emma, it was to advance more rapidly in math, even though she was already a full year ahead.

Emma's Chinese name was *Liu Zhenhe (or Tsenho) which* means precious peace; her pet name, Xiao Jiao (or *Shao-Chiau)* meant little intelligent one. Emma, child number seven of eight, and her one-year older brother, Luho, number six, were initially taught by a live-in tutor when their five older siblings went off to private schools. The tutor taught them Chinese, English, and Mathematics. After Luho moved to a more rigorous school, Emma was tutored with three boys from across the road (dressed as a boy to fit in.) She later took Luho's vacated previous place in his first private school, so as not to forfeit the prepaid tuition.

The next year Emma transferred to a school with much more advanced academics. She flourished there for five years; the first three were in coed classes but for the final two, she was transferred to an all-boys class of twenty students. So, thanks to her scholar father and progressive mother, in an era when education for girls was considered a waste of time, Emma landed in an elite class in the most competitive school in Hangzhou. She was not only the youngest student and only girl in the entire class, but also consistently ranked number one.

Enlin's tutoring and homeschooling allowed him to leapfrog grade levels, place out of subjects, and carry course overloads, compressing sixteen years of elementary through college into only twelve years. This unconventional educational achievement led to the unusual situation in which at age 14, he graduated from high school and at 17, was a professor of Chemistry, Math, and English at nearby colleges while his peers were still working to complete high school.

Emma received her bachelor's degree from Suzhou (Suchow) University (between Shanghai and Nanjing) in Sociology and was known for her strong academics, maturity, professional appearance, sensible shoes, plain clothes, and braided hair. After she wrapped up her master's degree, where her thesis dealt with the war-driven orphanage crises in large cities, she prepared to begin her PhD research, a very rare undertaking for women in China in those days. Just as she was about to begin her advanced program, she received an urgent request from the Shanghai Municipal Council on Child Services, beseeching her to immediately assume the Directorship of Shanghai's orphanages and implement the suggestions she had outlined in her thesis.

Emma's and Enlin's families had known each other socially in the mid 1920s and early 1930s in their hometown of Hangzhou. Emma's older sister, Zhou (Suho) married Enlin's younger brother "William" (Weilin), so the two families were connected by marriage as well. Emma was twelve years younger than Enlin, however, so they barely acknowledged each other growing up. She was immersed in her studies and writing during those early years while he was a successful banker in his twenties with the reputation of being "the most eligible bachelor in Shanghai." Emma's diary, however, hints that she had been well aware of this good-looking successful young man for some time. Even so, their early acquaintance did not flourish into a more romantic nature until Emma reached 23 and Enlin 35, the same ages that my wife and myself first met. We also married at the same ages (29 and 41).

Both Emma's and Enlin's parents came from aristocratic families who highly valued education. Their homes were supported by domestic servants, cooks, tutors, and seamstresses, as both fathers held prestigious professional positions. It was estimated that Emma's household had 30 servants who lived in a long back building along the creek. Both families were also forward thinking, concerned for the less fortunate and well aware of the realities of the rapidly changing world. Emma overheard her mother scold her father on more than one occasion for coming home coatless on a particularly cold day; he had given his fur coat away to a poor man shivering on a bench.

Over several years Emma's father evolved into a well-known thinker who published several books on philosophy. After his children were launched and wife comfortably settled, he made a significant life change. He burned his self-authored books, relinquished control of all his property, abandoned his family and retreated into the Hengshan mountains where he lived as a hermit serving others in the shadow of a Buddhist monastery for the rest of his life. His grave on Hengshan mountain, which my wife and her brother's family located in 2012, is still tended by local residents who continue to revere him and his good works.

1936
Emma, College Student

6.
IN CHARGE

Emma completed her bachelor's degree in sociology circa 1938 at Suzhou (Suchou) University, even as the city was being threatened with Japanese incursion during her senior year. There was little modern industry in Suzhou at the time, which was perhaps why it was of less interest to the Japanese than other, larger, neighboring industrialized cities.

Escalating war activities with the Japanese made Emma keenly aware of the "orphan problem." A vast number of children had been separated from their parents, either due to the chaos of panic-driven escapes, forced inscriptions, unidentifiable civilian collateral damage, or worse.

These newly orphaned children were streaming into Shanghai (fifty miles to the southeast of Suzhou) with no destination in mind. The charities, as well as the government welfare agencies, were totally overwhelmed and understaffed.

Although Shanghai itself had been under control of the Japanese since the battle of Shanghai in 1937, the International Zone, also called the International Settlement or the International Concession, was ruled by the Anglo-American Municipal Council until Dec 8, 1941 when it defaulted to Japanese control by simultaneously orchestrated attacks on Pearl Harbor, Hong Kong, and Singapore .

Emma discovered that not only did the Shanghai Municipal Council lack a consistent policy for processing these orphans, their staff had also been decimated over the last few years by the depletion of all its senior (male) associates.

Emma had drafted a master's thesis proposing a detailed restructuring of the whole orphan-handling process. Her paper made the rounds of her college department and unexpectedly resulted in a job offer from the government welfare agency in Shanghai. They requested her to postpone her PhD and implement her thesis immediately.

The paucity of qualified males and her advanced education in the field secured her offer. She was in the right place, at the right time, with the right credentials. At twenty-two, she was now in charge.

To carry out her new responsibilities, she moved to a relative's home in the French Concession (a contiguous area in Shanghai previously ruled by the French from Hanoi) with her mother, her uncle, and several extended family members.

7.
LOTS OF LIU'S

Emma's first order of business as the Director of the Social Welfare Agency with offices on the Bund was to introduce herself to her caseworkers and solicit their opinions and inputs concerning the operation of the present system and how it could be improved. These were the overworked, dedicated women on the front line who dealt with all the incoming "lost" children on a daily basis.

"It's their names," volunteered one caseworker. "So many of them don't have names. They're either too young to know or too traumatized to say them."

"Some," inserted a second caseworker, "insist their name is Didi (little brother), Meimei (little sister), or even Xiao Gou (little dog). It's not much to go on."

Emma made her first executive decision on the spot.

"Henceforth," she announced, "to add some order to this chaos, we will keep detailed records on where, when, and how each child is found, what they are wearing, and any other identification clues. All children whose names are unknown shall be assigned the name Liu."

"But that's your name!"

"Just as good as any other name. And besides, if our records get lost or destroyed, future generations will have somewhere to start should they try to trace their roots."

Result: there are still several hundred adults born in the mid to late 1930s with a family name Liu, who have no idea how they came by their names.

8.
WHERE OTHERS FEAR TO TREAD

—

1940

"I am sorry! I cannot! Please do not ask me to take him." With that, the caseworker broke into tears and rushed from the room.

Emma was speechless. All of her available case workers had responded similarly.

Emma turned to her assistant who had just entered her office. "Meiwen, I don't understand. There's something strange going on here. None of our caseworkers are willing to take on this new arrival. Has that ever happened before?."

"Not since I started working here. How strange. Are you referring to that new boy who was brought in late last night—the one that looks about six or seven and won't give his name? In fact, won't talk at all—barely nods his head when offered food or asked to follow?"

"That's the one. Can you snoop around a bit and see what's going on? If we're going to help this boy, we're going to need to learn what's behind the staff's reluctance to handle him."

The next morning Meiwen returned with her findings. "It seems our mystery boy is quite possibly the son of Du Yuesheng (one of the three major crime bosses in Shanghai at the time)."

Emma took pause. She knew what this information meant, that her staff would be fearful of this case due to the reputation of Du Yuesheng—the most dangerous mobster in all of Shanghai. She took a deep breath and made her decision.

"I know this sounds strange, Meiwen, but we are not unlike doctors. We treat everyone, regardless of who they are—good, bad, rich, or poor the same. But I don't want to traumatize my overworked staff, so I'll handle the boy myself. Where does Du Yuesheng hang out?"

"Probably in the red-light district on Fuzhou Road—but you can't go there! It's much too dangerous—thieves, thugs, kidnappers, rapists, murderers...."

"Well, if it's so dangerous, how on earth could I ask any of my staff to go there? No, it has to be me."

With this declaration, she grabbed the office bullhorn, and against the objections of her assistant who tried to block her path, scurried out of her office. Her assistant followed her down the corridor pleading, "Too dangerous! You're dressed too fancy. You'll be kidnapped—robbed, you...."

Emma caught a taxi and instructed the driver, "Take me to Fuzhou Road. Somewhere near Long Road."

"No! No! I cannot. Too dangerous! I will not take you."

"Alright then, just get me as close to there as you are willing. Then let me off."

From there she hired a rickshaw (pedicabs were not introduced into Shanghai until 1942) to bring her even closer to her destination, but then he too refused to go the last half mile. At this point she managed to bribe a truck driver to let her climb up into his truck bed. Once propped against the cab for stability, she pulled out her bullhorn and began soliciting the whereabouts of Du Yuesheng. Getting no response, she exited the rear of the truck once the driver approached her final destination as close as he dared and, armed with only her bullhorn, marched straight into the heart of the den of iniquity.

"Where can I find Du Yuesheng?" blared the bullhorn. "I need to talk to Du Yuesheng."

This spectacle elicited numerous smirks and stares but no responses, until suddenly, a well-dressed and well-mannered man of about forty confronted her. "Madam, pardon my intrusion but I must caution you. A refined lady like yourself should not be here—it's much too dangerous. Those three men over there—they've been following you and look like they mean you harm. Please let me arrange a safe escort away from this place to protect you before you get hurt or even worse."

"But I must find Du Yuesheng. Do you know where he is?"

"No, nobody does. He's the invisible man—he's never seen. But I do know someone who knows someone who might be able to get a message to him if you tell me what this is all about."

Emma decided to take a chance and explained, "I am the Director of the Social Welfare Agency. I believe I have found his son—a boy between six and eight. If the boy is truly his son, I wish to arrange for him to be reunited with his father."

"Perhaps I can help. In the meantime, these two friends of mine are totally trustworthy and can escort you out of here to a safe location."

"Thank you." With that, she gave the mystery man her card and retreated in the company of the two rather burly strangers assigned to her, too mentally exhausted by this time to worry about her own safety. Emotionally spent, Emma returned to her office. It had been four hours since her ordeal had begun. *I've done all I can*, she thought. *Now, it's only a matter of waiting.*

Emma's assistant spotted her as she returned to her office and, forgetting her station, ran up to her and almost hugged her. Then she pulled back, embarrassed. Her face, now a blotchy red, betrayed she had been crying for quite some time.

"I'm fine," Emma reassured her as she collapsed into her chair. Her assistant gave one last muffled cry of joy, clutched her handkerchief to her face, and retreated.

Two days later, an impeccably dressed man appeared at her office first thing in the morning and inquired about the boy.

"You do understand, don't you? I must think of the boy's safety first," explained Emma. "I must make sure you truly represent Du Yuesheng's interests and not that of his enemies who may attempt to kidnap the boy."

"Of course. I appreciate your position. Send for the boy and I'll prove to you that I am known to him."

The boy was brought to her office by her assistant. He spotted the stranger and immediately ran to him shouting, "Uncle, Uncle!" This was the first word anyone at the Agency had heard him speak.

"Ok. I'm satisfied. Thank you for coming to retrieve him. Please take good care of him. As taciturn as he has been, I've actually grown quite fond of him."

The boy turned toward her, and true to form, said nothing, but gave her a huge, unexpected smile, then turned, clasped the hand of his "Uncle", and disappeared from her office and from her life.

9.
BUT WAIT, THERE'S MORE

Emma quickly immersed herself in the problems at hand and thought no more of the boy or his uncle. However, that was about to change.

"That guy's back," Meiwen whispered to Emma in her office a week later.

"What guy?"

"That fancy dressed guy who claimed to be the boy's uncle."

"Oh dear, what does he want? I thought this matter was over and done with. Well then, you might as well show him in—let's find out what he wants."

"Ah, Miss Liu, thank you for seeing me."

"How may I help you? I'm assuming the boy is happy with his present situation."

"Yes. Father and son are both very happy. Both shed many tears when they were reunited. The reason I'm here is to thank you for your kindness in a more substantial manner."

"What do you mean? I don't understand."

"What do you want? Money, jewelry? Du Yuesheng wishes to thank you with a gift, a token of his appreciation for what you did for him and his son. Anything, anything at all."

"Want? No, this is my job. I do it out of love for the children. I want nothing else, but please thank Du Yuesheng for his generous offer."

"Nothing? You must want something. Everyone wants something!" The boy's uncle could not help betraying his expression of disbelief. Her response was truly unexpected. *What kind of woman is this,* he thought, *especially in desperate times like these.* He inquired once again but was met with the same response.

As the man rose and reached the door to leave, Emma caught herself.

"Wait! Wait a moment. There is something you can do. But it may be beyond even Du Yuesheng's power."

"Try me."

"This war, the occupation. It's all so horrible. The men—husbands, sons, fathers— all gone, either with the government, the army, on the run, or captured. It's an enormous burden on the women left behind, particularly mothers of small children. These women must fend for themselves. Often their only alternative is to work long hours in the sweatshops. With so many extended families in disarray, they have no choice but to depend on daycare, daycare which we provide."

"I don't understand. What are you getting at? Might I remind you, Miss Lui—we are not in the daycare business."

"Let me explain. We've established many daycare centers throughout the city to address these women's needs, but it's hard to keep staff. And why is that? It's too dangerous. They're waylaid by bandits, robbed of what little they have, beaten, and sometimes even raped. Two of our caretakers were murdered last month. These women are very vulnerable and easy targets."

"So what do you want from me?"

"Protection. Real protection! It's probably too big a problem to fix, but anything, anything at all you can do to help would benefit every one of us."

The man sat thinking for a moment, then rose to leave. As he reached the door, he turned towards Emma and added, "Can't promise anything, but I'll see what can be done."

A week later Emma made her rounds of the daycare centers starting with one located in a particularly dangerous neighborhood. *What are those men doing on the corner?* she thought. *Looks like they're holding guns! I hope everyone's okay at the daycare.* She crossed the street to keep as much distance between her and these threatening strangers as she could and then slipped through the side door of the center unnoticed.

As she entered, the local daycare director ran up to her. "Miss Liu, Miss Liu! You won't believe what has happened. Three days ago, we had a visitor. A well-dressed man who came in to inform us that the reign of terror for daycare workers is over. He said the word is out. Anyone harassing a daycare worker will suffer grave circumstances—we are now officially protected. I have no idea how or by whom but frankly, I don't care. But isn't that wonderful? My staff can breathe more easily now. We're safe."

"Is that why I saw those men with guns on the corner?"

"I think so. There was a confrontation with some thugs when they started to harass one of our workers two days ago. Our protectors got rather rough with them, but all's quiet now."

Emma was to find similar stories all over the city. Problem solved—all because of one boy who wouldn't talk. Emma smiled to herself but told no one "the how, the why, or the by whom" of this miracle which lay dormant for over fifty years until she shared her story with me and her daughter one late evening in the comfort of her own home.

If Du Yuesheng were indeed the Shanghai crime boss in this story, he contributed to Emma's "protect the daycare workers" campaign in another way as well. As ruthless and brutal as Du Yuesheng was, he was reputed to have one saving grace—his directive that all gang members treat women with respect. So it appears that of all the mob bosses, he would have been the one most sympathetic to Emma's cause.

In Shanghai, the French Concession remained relatively intact, probably because Germany, a Japanese ally, had occupied France since July 1940, seventeen months earlier. Residing in the French Concession worked to Emma's advantage and made it easier for her group to make their escape.

11.
FLEEING SHANGHAI

The Japanese carried out an amphibious invasion on Hangzhou Bay during the late summer of 1937. In anticipation of Hangzhou's probable occupation, Emma's family had sold many of their valuables to increase their liquidity. These included Ming porcelains, precious books, and rare scrolls—all for a small fraction of their true value. What they could not easily and quickly sell, they buried, in hopes that they could be recovered sometime after the war was over (these items were never recovered). With the proceeds from the sales of the more valuable items, they purchased a large number of quality gems, which they had sewn by their family seamstress into the hems of their less fancy everyday garments—garments that would not betray their upper-class status. When traveling in such dangerous times, they wanted to appear as invisible as possible. It was unlikely that they spent the gems directly. More likely they sold the gems one at a time, converting their value to a more spendable, lower density currency such as silver or copper coins; some of the family moved to Shanghai.

Emma's father had become a hermit in the mountains several years prior to this event so he was out of touch with both the family and the war. At a family conference on the night of the Japanese takeover of Shanghai's International Zone on Dec. 8, 1941, Emma put the critical question to Muma (her mother). "Muma, what should we do? The Shanghai

International Zone is no longer a sanctuary for us. It cannot provide protection. We have nowhere to hide. The Japanese are arresting everyone that they think might be a threat to them and taking them away. No one knows where. Do we run, or do we stay?"

Her mother stood up straight and with clenched fists declared firmly, "No child of mine shall ever work for the enemy—under any circumstances!"

That was enough for Emma, but the group as a whole remained divided. Those members of the family who feared the Japanese reputation for cruel and sadistic treatment of their enemies, including Emma and her mother, took their share of the gems and prepared to leave. The others decided to take their chances and remain behind. In the final vote, eight (including Emma and her mother) chose to flee.

December 12th, four days later, Emma and the other seven members of her party wrapped up their affairs and set off for Guilin (Kweilin), just under a thousand miles by road/path/river in the southwestern region of China's Interior. Their objective was to reach Chonqing (Chungking), the provisional wartime capital of Free China beyond Japanese control.

Their little gang of eight comprised of Emma (twenty-four at the time), Muma, Paoho (Emma's younger sister), her "uncle" (actually a family friend), Zhenhai, (her four-year-old nephew), Zhang Naima (her nephew's nurse), Luho (Emma's older brother), and Zhou Sanlo (a friend of Luho's). They were ill-equipped to tackle such an arduous and treacherous journey, and in retrospect, the odds of their succeeding were miniscule. What they considered to be the even greater danger, the danger of remaining in Shanghai, propelled them to ignore the odds and set off on their perilous journey.

They first made their way on foot to the small Suzhou Creek, north of Shanghai Central, where they hired a canal boat to begin their escape. Emma felt it was much safer to use this less conspicuous river route rather than the busy Huangpu River which flowed through Shanghai proper. Every time there was a chance they might be spotted from a guard post while passing under a bridge, they would scrunch low down under a tarp to avoid detection.

Emma's mother had bound feet, befitting a high-class aristocrat of the early twentieth century, so Emma and the other adults took turns carrying her on their backs when the trails were too rough for her to negotiate or when other modes of transportation were unavailable. Her inept "uncle" tried to dictate their travel strategy, but after a few weeks of witnessing his poor critical thinking skills and trying to placate him, Emma finally mandated that he should either stay out of the way or fend for himself. By even her young age of twenty-four, Emma had already endured more than her share of tough leadership challenges under difficult conditions. She had evolved into a strong and competent take-charge woman.

They traveled inland for many weeks, alternating among boats, buses, rickshaws, walking, and the backs of open trucks, using whatever mode of transportation they could muster, provided it took them mostly southwestward. They spent their nights in small hovel-like hotels along the journey to avoid drawing attention to themselves. They found it easier to travel unnoticed than they had anticipated, for the roads were crowded with refugees heading in both directions so one more family of eight hardly made a difference—especially one that included an elderly woman and a four-year old boy.

Finally, after nearly four months of close calls enduring terrible conditions, they reached a village close to a boundary lake region separating the Chinese and Japanese-held territories (a no man's land). The complex terrain consisted of numerous marshy lakes interconnected by blind narrow canals—navigable only by the experienced local fishermen. The Japanese soldiers guarding this section of border were lightly armed as the area was considered neither strategic nor suitable for heavy equipment.

The group rested for a week to assess the local situation as Emma devised a plan. Using some of their remaining gem-currency, she hired three guides, each with a narrow skiff designed specifically to wend through the local maze of narrow canals. Each skiff could hold up to four adults (including the guide) seated in a single file. Emma hoped their guides could be trusted to convey them across the boundary lake to Free China.

They shoved off as night fell and traveled in silence. Most of the early guard checkpoints were abandoned, so progress was relatively uneventful until they passed under the final footbridge. There, the canal opened out into the large expanse of the main lake.

A Japanese guard, stationed at this last check point, challenged the first boat from the middle of the bridge above, "Where are you going? Where are your papers? You must show me your papers! I'll not let you pass without proper papers."

The nurse in the first boat, having been coached by Emma, replied, "Oh sir, we are taking our invalid grandmother to her daughter. She is old and quite ill, and only her daughter is able to care for her. Our papers are all together in a boat behind us."

The second boat was also challenged, but like the first, was able to convince the guard that their papers too were in the third trailing boat, so it passed through as well.

"Ah, you are the last boat. You must have everyone's papers! Right?"

Emma replied, "Oh yes sir, they are right here."

"Bring them to me."

"Sir, my leg is badly injured, and I am unable to stand. I cannot do so."

"You must!"

"I would, sir, if I were able, but I cannot walk. I am sorry sir. You must climb down here to see them."

"Can't you see," he responded angrily, "I'm in the middle of doing my business! I can't come down. Do you think I don't know what you're up to? I see your kind all the time—trying to trick me. Well, it won't work. You're crossing the lake to smuggle contraband back to this side of the lake."

"Oh no sir, we would never do such a thing. That would be against the law."

"You better believe it—and with harsh penalties. I'll not listen to your lies. I demand one-fifth of everything you bring back as your penalty for being so disrespectful to a Japanese officer. This is your only way back, so you have no choice. I'll be waiting. You understand? **Do you understand?**"

"Oh yes sir, I understand."

"Off with you then. I'll be watching for you, so don't try any tricks."

(Emma was an elegant lady of 80 when she told me this story and could not bring herself to use the vernacular as spoken by the soldier, but we all knew what she meant.)

They passed through the last obstacle to freedom.

1942
Enlin and Emma Together at Last in Chungking

12.
REACHING FREE CHINA

Once they reached the far side of the lake early next morning, they were intercepted by Chinese soldiers and escorted to a local headquarters. There, they were greeted most graciously by a senior officer. "Miss Liu, welcome. We have been expecting you."

"But how could you possibly know I was coming?"

The senior officer laughed. "Mr. Pan has followed your progress as best he could and has alerted everyone along your probable route to keep an eye out for you. He's quite resourceful you know."

"Yes, I know."

Emma could not help but to smile to herself thinking how much of an understatement the officer's remarks really were.

"But forgive me. You must be exhausted after your long journey. Arrangements have been made for you to be taken into town where hotel rooms await you and your companions as soon as you are ready." The little group rested there for a few days and from there completed their eventful journey in provided vehicles.

Emma's fiancé, Mr. Enlin Pan, exercised his long arm of influence to safeguard her travel through Free China. He was, after all, President of the China Travel Service and controlled not only a vast number of the hotels in China but also the railroads and airways.

That first night Emma was shown her room, she was a bit taken aback. After her several-month torturous journey, she anticipated a somewhat higher level of comfort now that they had finally reached Free China. Surprise, her room had no bed! She managed to improvise by placing a few scattered boards across two chairs. She finally fell asleep when a knock at the door announced the arrival of three young soldiers—a captain with two young privates in tow.

"Miss," they began rather briskly, "we have come to inspect your luggage. It is mandatory that we examine the personal effects of all new arrivals. A matter of security."

"Certainly. I only have this one small suitcase—I haven't even unpacked yet."

She watched them closely as they removed the contents of her suitcase. They treated each item as a delicate piece of porcelain. When they came upon her undergarments, they slowly morphed. No longer were they soldiers—they were boyfriends, husbands, brothers, and lovers—all with wet eyes grateful for even the briefest reminder of their loved ones, so long unseen, so far away.

"Everything seems to be in order. Thank you, Miss." The captain's voice was perceptibly softer this time.

"No trouble. I understand you can't be too careful in times like these."

With that, the captain saluted and left with his two underlings.

An hour later a new group of soldiers, four this time, embarked on the same routine. This process was repeated a few more times until finally, at three in the morning, she gained enough solitude to get a few hours of sleep.

Fifty years later when she shared her story with her family, she explained, "These young soldiers were so homesick, so worried about their loved ones—who was I to deny them some small comfort, some solace, some remembrance, some hope?"

13.
"IT WAS THE WHITE DRESS"

"My, what a pretty white dress!"

"Thank you. It's my favorite. My mother had it made especially for my 24th birthday. I wear it every time I get a chance because I love it so much. But I do worry it might get dirty."

Thus began the casual conversation between an elegant middle-aged lady and Emma, her young seat companion, as their train pulled out of the Guilin (Kweilin) train station to begin the 325-mile journey northeast to Changsha (Ch'ang-sha) in Hunan province in the late spring of 1942.

"And what takes you to Changsha during such turbulent times?" the older woman inquired. "It's getting to be a very dangerous city, you know, now that the Japanese have taken over the Shanghai International Zone—and that's only 675 miles further north of Changsha. Too close for my comfort. Who knows where they'll strike next!"

"My brother."

"Your brother?"

"Yes, Wuho, my older brother."

"Oh, your brother lives in Changsha then?"

"No, not there. He lives up in the southern Hengshan mountain. It'll take me another full day by bus to reach him—starting tomorrow. He is quite ill with TB exacerbated by an old riding accident that never healed properly."

"Goodness, how dreadful."

"Yes, he was thrown from his horse while trying to jump over a fallen tree in his path. My mother asked if I could bring him medicine, a modern type not available at the remote monastery where he is convalescing. I added a few treats to give him a break from the bland monastic fare and slipped in a few family photos to cheer him up."

Emma and seven companions (her mother, younger sister, one older brother and his friend, uncle, young nephew, and nephew's wet nurse) had recently escaped Shanghai and traveled as refugees for several months to reach safety in Guilin. They had started their dramatic and dangerous journey to Free China a few days after Pearl Harbor, Singapore, and Manila were attacked. The Japanese simultaneously took control of the Shanghai International Zone. Shortly after their little band of seven reached the relative safety of Guilin, they received word that another of Emma's older brothers, Wuho, was seriously ill up in the mountains, nearly 500 miles northeast of Guilin, halfway back towards Shanghai. Emma's mother was well aware there were no modern doctors in that remote part of the country, so her son would be desperate without some form of family assistance.

She asked Emma if she would be willing to transport some modern medicines to her brother, which were more effective at easing his suffering than the herbal remedies dispensed by local healers. They all knew the journey would be quite perilous, and no one would blame her if she chose not to go. Without the slightest hesitation, Emma accepted the challenge, and now found herself on a train bound for Changsha, chatting away with her new friend. (On such an arduous journey, she may in fact have been accompanied by a servant or a family friend part of the way who might not have been considered a companion.)

"I myself am heading to Changsha to take care of my ailing mother. She had a stroke, and her doctor says she needs constant care for at least six months. Otherwise, I'd stay put in Guilin far away from harm's way. If all goes well, I'll bring her back home with me in the spring."

"I'm so sorry to hear about your mother."

"Thank you. I'm afraid it's all to be expected though. She'll be ninety in a few months. But tell me dear, I do hope you have someone meeting you in Changsha. It's quite unsafe these days for a single young girl, particularly one as pretty as you, to be wandering around those streets alone."

"Oh yes. Uncle will meet me and put me up for the night. Then I'm off in the morning to the mountains, about 125 miles from Changsha. With no complications, I should be able get to my brother's place in one more day—there are no trains, only unreliable buses at best—we'll see."

"Do you take this trip often?"

"Actually, I haven't seen him for several years. It will be good to see him again—even though he is ill."

"Well then, this certainly is a special occasion, and your lovely white dress is perfect. Is that package you're carrying for him?"

"Yes. His medicine, treats, and personal items."

Several hours later the world changed. A Japanese squadron returning from a raid chanced upon Emma's train.

The pilots had not expended their entire ordnance on their previous targets. According to protocol, should they encounter an enemy target of opportunity upon their return, they were to engage and inflict as much damage as possible with what munitions they had left. The train they came upon, directly along their flight path, presented just such an opportunity. Without hesitation, they initiated their attack and dropped their bombs.

Utter pandemonium broke out on the train as it screeched to a halt.

The onboard military personnel guarding the train decided that the passengers were at great risk if they remained onboard and ordered: "Everyone out! Quick, to the ditches! You will be safer there. The Japanese want to destroy the train and don't care about you. Out, out, out! Hurry! Now!"

Most passengers complied, while a few, frozen with fear, refused to vacate their seats; people scattered in all directions, driven by panic. One young lady, however, looked aghast at how the muddy the ditches contrasted with her clean white dress and decided: *there is no way a few stupid Japanese fighter-bombers are going to make me get my dress dirty.*

Emma ignored the soldiers' orders. She grabbed her brother's parcel, broke loose from the soldier trying to help her, and took off running in the opposite direction up the hill. The soldier's shouts of concern had no effect, she just kept running. She made for the lone tree halfway to the top, hoping it would afford her at least some protection from the attackers. She clung to the tree whose cover in fact, did offer her some refuge. The white dress, however, in contrast to the surrounding ground cover, stood out as an obvious target to one approaching plane. This plane made a particularly low pass and released a large bomb most adroitly on target.

"Thud!"

The young lady stared directly at the undetonated, partially buried, large bomb not more than 20 feet in front of her. It was a dud, or *was it*, she thought. Now she contemplated a new conundrum. *Do I run from the bomb and expose myself to further attack from the planes, or stay here and if the bomb changes its mind, be blown to bits?*

The more she thought about it, the more obvious the answer seemed. *If the bomb hasn't exploded in the last twenty seconds, it's unlikely to explode in the next twenty seconds.* Twenty seconds later, *If it hasn't exploded in the last forty seconds, it's unlikely to explode in the next forty seconds. If it hasn't exploded...*

Within five minutes the planes had expended the last of their ordnance, including their complete store of high caliber machine gun ammunition. They vanished. Screams and moans emanated from the ditches. The majority of people who had sought shelter there were now either dead or seriously wounded—due to the planes strafing straight down the ditch.

The survivors were somehow able to cut loose the rear few cars that had suffered the most severe damage. This left the engine and the front few cars sufficiently intact to continue. The crippled train, disabled as it was and crammed with survivors, limped on. Eventually, the true hero-train (I think I can, I think I can…) pulled into the station, eight hours behind schedule and missing several cars. Emma rode out the last few hours of the trip curled up in a tiny ball in the corner of her seat clutching her brother's package. Somehow it comforted her, knowing she could still complete her mission.

Not until the train neared its destination did she realize that her kind companion was nowhere to be seen; her seat was occupied by someone else. "And I don't even know her name," she said out loud to herself. She reflected, *to lose a friend is tragic but to not even know her name is more so.*

When the train pulled into the station, the scene was utter chaos. There were fewer than a hundred surviving passengers, but the station was jammed with medical personnel, soldiers, local officials and several hundred relatives all hoping, above hope, to find their loved ones among the survivors. Emma got off the train but just stood there. It was all so hazy in her brain. She was stunned by so many frantic people shedding tears—a few laughing with joy as they hugged their loved ones, but the vast majority crying in despair.

Emma's uncle was there straining to find Emma in what seemed to be an endless swirling sea of humanity. Then he spotted her. He couldn't actually see her face but somehow, he knew it was she. "Emma, Emma, Emma!" he shouted. She thought she heard someone call her name above the deafening din, but wasn't sure. Then just as she turned to check, her uncle wrapped his arms around her with tears streaming down his face and excitedly choked out, "You're safe! Oh my god, you're safe! Up to a few hours ago, we had been told everyone on the train had perished. Then we heard there were a few survivors, and they were on their way. We all gathered here—each hoping our people were among the living." He took the parcel she had clung onto so tightly for the last many hours from her shaking hands and led the traumatized young Emma away from the crowd.

"It was the white dress," she murmured as they proceeded to her uncle's home. "Mother would have been so upset if I let my white dress get dirty. It was the white dress. Mother's present protected me. She saved me with the white dress." Emma explained to her uncle how the white dress motivated her to hide under the tree on the hill. How it kept the bomb from exploding. Her uncle listened intently, then he couldn't help but add, "Emma, it was more than that."

"What do you mean, more?"

"I was convinced I would never find you at the station even if you were one of the survivors actually on the train. So many people! So long since I've last seen you. So much confusion and shouting. Then, among all the confusion, I saw an angel. I saw a bright white shining angel glowing from the crowd. Somehow, I knew it was you. It was your mother's gift to you, the white dress, that guided me to you."

As he brought her to his home, he strongly urged that she return to Guilin as soon as she could and give up the remaining leg of her pilgrimage. "It's much too dangerous," he insisted. But she too insisted, "This may be the last time I'll ever see Wuho alive—I have to continue. I must bring him his medicine and his treats." After two days of rest, the strong young woman prevailed, continued on her journey, and succeeded in her quest. She stayed to care for Wuho in a small cottage attached to the monastery for a full month before she headed back to Guilin. Her premonition was correct, however. She never saw her brother again after that last eventful trip.

Her return to Guilin was relatively free of danger, although she did hold her breath as her train passed through the area of the previous attack, now strewn with abandoned railcar carcasses.

All the while during her return, she knew she would be safe—after all, she was wearing the White Dress.

試場規則

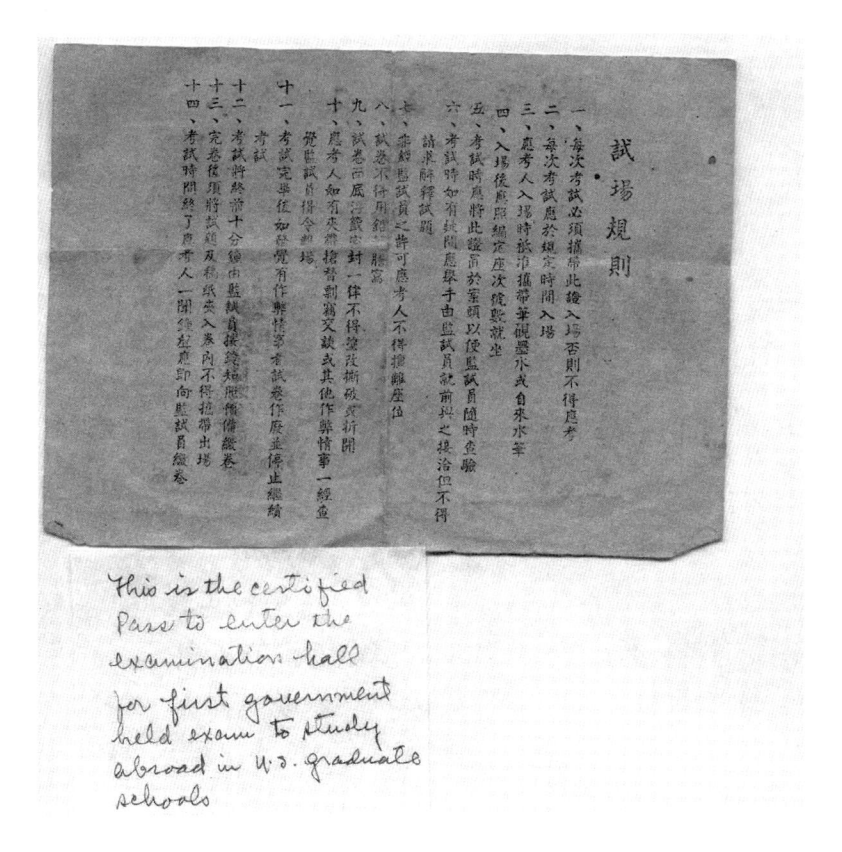

1、每次考試必須攜帶此證入場否則不得應考
2、每次考試應於規定時間入場
3、應考人入場時祗准攜帶筆硯墨水或自來水筆
4、入場後照編定座次燒數就坐
5、考試時將此證當於案頭以便監試員隨時查驗
6、考試時如有疑問應舉手由監試員就前科之接洽但不得請求解釋試題
7、非經患試員之許可應考人不得擅離座位
8、試卷不得作記號
9、試卷而屬二類者封一律不得發落撕破或折開
10、應考人如有夾帶搶替剝竊又讀或其他作弊情事一經查覺監試員得令出場
11、考試完畢徵如發覺有作弊情事者試卷作廢並停止繼續
12、考試將終帶十分鐘由監試員搖鈴預備繳卷
13、完卷後須將試題及試紙卷內不得挾帶出場
14、考試時間終了恩考人一聞鈴聲應即向監試員繳卷

This is the certified Pass to enter the examination hall for first government held exam to study abroad in U.S. graduate schools

1943
Emma's International Grad School
Exam Pass

14.

THE HUMP

—

CHINA TO INDIA

Mr. Enlin Pan, as Executive Vice President of the Shanghai Commercial Bank, was sent as the bank's representative to the U.S. to attend the 1944 International Business Conference in Rye, New York (featured as the Newsweek cover, October 1944). He remained in his position as head of Shanghai Commercial Bank's New York office until the Communists closed China six years later, at which point his position was eliminated. He was initially forced to leave Emma behind until they could manage to bring her out as well. They planned to meet and marry in the U.S. as soon as they could, but given the complexities of the war, they were weak on details.

Luckily, even at the height of the war, the Nationalist government who represented Free China, realized it behooved them to lay the groundwork they would need to rebuild the country once hostilities ended. Their long-term plan included creating a countrywide examination to select a cadre of young scholars who would travel to the U.S. to attend graduate schools. The examination was restricted to outstanding young scholars who had earned, at a minimum, an undergraduate college degree in an identified field of study. The year Emma took the examination, the top scoring 240 participants, 198 men and 42 women, were chosen.

Emma took the test and waited—with all fingers and toes crossed. She was nervous because she had been out of the academic world for more than two years and felt she was too rusty to compete effectively. She hoped. She waited. She hoped some more.

A month later the results were posted. It was two weeks more of agonizing wait before her cousin was able to get the official results. POW! Prayers answered. She stared at the telegram in disbelief. Not only did she make the list, she was the top woman scholar!

Before leaving for America, however, all selectees were required to attend a Nationalist military boot camp high in the mountains for a month of military training. The Nationalists believed members of this elite group might be derailed by their experiences in America and corrupted away from the Party's way of thinking. Emma, for what she considered to be a wasted month of her life, was compelled to wear an army uniform, march every day, listen to hours of lectures, learn to shoot, and sleep with a gun under her bed. Her conclusion was, "What's the point?"

Finding transportation to America after she completed her month of training was her next obstacle. With Enlin's help, she finally gained passage on a small convoy of three U.S. troop transports set to leave from India and return to San Pedro/Long Beach, California.

Yet one seemingly unresolvable obstacle remained—reaching the coast of India, on the other side of the Himalayas. As difficult as it was to cross the Himalayas, passing overland through Burma would have been even more difficult and certainly far more dangerous.

After Emma stood by for several weeks, Enlin finally managed to secure her a highly prized seat on a two engine C-47 that flew the Hump (the nickname for the Himalayas) twice a week between China and India. The plane flew a different, rather circuitous route each time to keep its routes as unpredictable as possible and to avoid Japanese detection.

Emma was the only female passenger on the flight. Her important-looking companions were all quite taciturn and barely acknowledged each other, much less her, an insignificant woman.

They probably think I'm Chiang Kai-shek's mistress, she mused to herself. *Well fine. At least that'll give them something to think about besides the war.*

It was a particularly turbulent and tortuous flight, with the internal cabin temperature plunging to well below zero and flight altitudes that occasionally strayed above sixteen thousand feet without oxygen. (The service ceiling of a C-47 is 26,400 feet.) These planes were designed with canvas bench seats facing each other across the aisle for utilitarian use, not for comfort. None of the passengers, restrained with harnesses, escaped the hardships of the journey. Most of them vomited, were subjected to severe bruising due to the unpredictable crosswinds, and nearly all suffered some form of frostbite and/or altitude sickness.

Emma, being young and strong, fared better than most of the other passengers and tried to replace thoughts of her considerable suffering with the relief she knew that would come once she reached India—and then the ultimate joy when she and Enlin would be permanently reunited in California.

1944

Emma's Ship Pass to California

15.
EMMA BOUND FOR AMERICA

–

1945

The three ships that made up Emma's convoy ferried troops and war supplies to support the war-staging areas in India. They then returned to Long Beach to repeat the cross Pacific supply trek. Emma and the other women also heading to the U.S. were assigned quarters on the middle ship. None of the passengers were told what, if anything, was being ferried in the first and third ships. They guessed of course, but it was all speculation.

Ironically, Enlin had traveled on one of these very same ships when he traveled to the U.S. more than a year earlier and was able to get a letter to Emma before her departure. In it he described the conditions she should expect, the personal items she could buy on board, and the items she should stock up on before departing. Thus, Emma was better prepared for this arduous journey than most of her fellow passengers.

The ships were not designed for comfort but did have adequate resources aboard to accommodate the passengers during their several week transit. The all women dorm cabin to which Emma had been assigned was packed with several rows of triple level bunks, each with an assigned personal storage locker. These lockers were designed to hold the gear of one combat-ready soldier, so Emma's locker proved sufficient for her meager belongings, including those recommended by Enlin that she acquired in India.

Communal showers and toilets were located a short distance down the corridor on the same level. Scheduled simple meals were provided in the troop mess for the women three times a day on a rotating schedule.

The women were told the voyage would take approximately six weeks, so they organized and "made homey" their quarters as best they could. The convoy left Calcutta, India and headed due south until they reached the frigid waters of the Antarctic Ocean. Then they headed due east, passing south of Australia to minimize the dangers posed by marauding Japanese submarines. This strategy had worked in the past and almost worked this time—almost.

BOOM

A large explosion was heard near dusk. Word quickly spread that the first ship in the convoy had been torpedoed and was listing severely. Several additional explosions signaled the likely demise of the first ship.

A few minutes later, Emma's middle ship was jolted by the loudest explosion yet. The women in her room were frightened but didn't panic. These women were survivors. They had all endured more than their share of life-threatening hardships and had grown accustomed to facing danger with patience, perseverance, and courage.

Fortunately, the damage to Emma's middle ship from the single hit was not crippling. Several additional explosions indicated the third ship, like the first, had not been so lucky. Later Emma learned that both the first ship and third ship had been sunk. The Japanese submarine broke off its engagement before it could return its attention to the middle ship—for reasons unknown.

The only casualty in Emma's dorm was an eight month pregnant woman who had been propelled off her top bunk onto the floor by the hit to their ship; she began to go into labor. A dozen women rushed to her aid. The mother was badly bruised, but nothing was broken. The baby meanwhile, unaware that her entrance into the world was unconventional, took it all in stride. She looked as healthy as if she had been born in the fanciest hospital in the world.

The twenty or so new "aunties" rifled through their personal effects, and without a second thought, ripped their slips apart to form diapers for the comfort of the new arrival—probably the only time in history a baby was born at sea with the luxury of all-silk diapers.

Compared to her previous tumultuous travel hazards including her train being bombed and strafed, her late night escape from the Shanghai International Zone, her traverse of Japanese-occupied China while caring for seven dependents, her outrageous bluff of a Japanese guard to cross the war zone border into Free China, flying over the Hump, surviving the Japanese submarine attack on her U.S. bound convoy, the rest of her voyage from Australia to California was like summer camp.

Enlin met Emma's ship at the San Pedro pier near Long Beach, where they were finally reunited. Finally together. Finally about to begin their new life together.

They first visited USC for a few days where Emma had been accepted into graduate school in sociology to work on her PhD. Due to her unscheduled delay, she was unable to enroll in her program upon her arrival and was asked to wait a few months to begin her program. She did, however, audit a few classes to get a better understanding of what attending graduate school at USC would entail.

Shortly thereafter, in mid-January, 1945, Emma and Enlin headed north to San Francisco where they tied the knot on January 20, 1945 in the First Congregational Church at the corner of Post and Mason. They honeymooned in the St. Francis Hotel half a block away on Union Square, then traveled cross-country to New York City by train to begin their thirty-three year life together while she waited for her USC program to begin. (Ironically, as I write this part of their 77 year old story, I can look down from the fifteenth floor of the Club Donatello Hotel in San Francisco directly across Mason Street on the church, now part of the San Francisco Art Academy, in which they were married.)

Over the next two years, circumstances intervened, which changed Emma's plans about attending graduate school. The lovebirds opted to start a family instead.

1945
Emma Expecting First Child

1946
Emma-New York Style

16.
MATERNAL FAMILY TRADITION

–

FLIGHT AND SURVIVAL

1) Emma's Great Grandmother fled her burning compound with Emma's three-year old grandmother secured to her back with silk scarves and lowered them over the city wall to escape into the countryside during Taiping Rebellion in 1853.

2) Emma's Grandmother was lowered over the city wall, captured and released by Taiping rebels. She died sixty years later shortly after joining her daughter (Emma's mother) during the overthrow of the Qing dynasty in 1911.

3) Emma's mother made military mavericks back down from seizing their home during the Qing dynasty revolution while mourning the death of both her mother and infant son. She fled Shanghai with Emma following the Japanese takeover and crossed Japanese-controlled China to Guilin where she succumbed to illness.

4) After Emma's Dec 11th, 1941 escape from Shanghai, she bluffed a Japanese guard to pass through no man's land to reach Free China.

5) She stared down an undetonated bomb during a Japanese air attack on her train (circa 1942) and endured a four-month dangerous trek across Japanese occupied-China (carrying her mother who had bound feet, part of the time on her back.) She survived the high altitude flight over "The Hump," and made her way to America on the only surviving ship in a three-ship convoy attacked by a Japanese submarine in 1944.

ENLIN PAN,
FATHER-IN-LAW

1943
Enlin in Chongqing (Chungking)

1943
Emma Takes a Ride

1945
Enlin-International Businessman

17.
PAN FAMILY HISTORY

Two Families Overview

Both Emma Liu (1917-2011) and Enlin Pan (1905-1978) came from upper class families in Hangzhou, a large ancient city founded around 600 CE, 110 miles southwest of Shanghai. These two families were related through marriage, as Enlin's younger brother, Weilin (William), was married to Emma's older sister, Zhou (Suho). But as Emma was twelve years younger than Enlin, their initial relationship was that of a serious teenage girl and an incredibly accomplished young man of the world who barely acknowledged her existence.

He was smitten (or as he later confessed to his children, "My heart was stirred"), when he later noticed the mature sixteen-year old perched over her books at her sunlit desk in her family's home. Their romance did not fully blossom until Emma reached twenty-three and Enlin thirty-five. Before Cupid showed up to do his thing, Enlin pursued his own life path, getting unhappily married at too young an age, fathering three children, separating over a scandal regarding his then-wife, and eventually divorcing—all before thirty-five.

Enlin's non-domestic accomplishments fared far better during his teens and early twenties. He whizzed through high school, entered college at fourteen and graduated at seventeen with a BS in Chemistry. One of his early responsibilities was as the English translator for Dr. Sun Yat-sen when he was in the vicinity, a decade after Dr. Sun's two-month tenure as the provisional President of the Republic of China (January 1 - March 10, 1912). Dr. Sun was considered the founding father of modern China and is still revered by Chinese on both the Mainland and Taiwan. At seventeen, Enlin accepted a position as a professor of English at University of Shanghai.

He was also a professor of Chemistry, Math, and English at the Northeastern University in Manchuria and the National University of Chekiang in Hangzhou before switching to the post office and then banking. He served as Director of the Shanghai Commercial Bank, President of China Travel Services, and headed the foreign division of Railway Supply and Manufacturing Company in Ohio. He also served as President of Central Media, a Scripps Howard computer company in New York City and eventually as a trusted advisor to the Shing Kwan Investment and Shipping company in Hong Kong and Singapore.

Pan Yuan Po (Enlin's Grandfather, 1840-1899)

Pan Yuan Po, Enlin's grandfather, was born in Hangzhou, Zhejiang (Chekiang) Province, China during the reign of Dao Kwan (1821-1850, Qing Dynasty). He married well to Miss Shin, sister of Shih Hsiang-Chai, the Vice Chancellor of Suzhou (Soochow) University.

Pan Yuan Po was in the first graduating class of the Guan Qi (Kwang Chi) Medical School in Hangzhou. He specialized in treating opium addicts, mostly Manchu officials in Hangzhou, who wanted to be free from their drug habit. This proved to be a propitious career choice, and he became quite prosperous, which afforded him "the good life." His definition of "the good life" included women (he most likely took on a mistress), a garden populated with an abundance of peacocks, and an array of beautiful orchards throughout their property.

Yuan Po and Shin produced five children, four girls and Enlin's father, Pan Shi-Chao. Due to Yuan Po's philandering, Shin turned to Christianity for comfort and devoted much of her life's work to the church. She was a modern woman and unlike the fashion of the day, did not have bound feet.

Pan Shi-Chao (Enlin's Father, 1878-1966)

Pan Shi-Chao, also named Pan Chung-Chau (according to custom, a man often had two names), was born in Hangzhou and died of a stroke in Shanghai at 88. He married Miss Soong Tzu Tsen (1880-1934) in 1901, Enlin's mother also from Hangzhou. When Su-tsen, who was old fashioned and had bound feet, was first introduced to her new mother and three sisters-in-law, modern women without bound feet, a cultural rift immediately formed between them, which never fully healed.

After their honeymoon, the young couple settled down in Hangzhou to start a family. Meanwhile Shi-Chao decided to take the civil exam to enter the Postal Service. He scored well and was named Postmaster of various cities throughout Chekiang Provence. The couple had two sons and two daughters: Mei-Ju (Mildred, Enlin's older sister), Enlin, Meili (Mary),

And Weilin (William married Emma's elder sister, Suho and died at a young age in a motorcycle accident, leaving his widow with three young children.)

Shi-Chao loved Enlin the most of his four children and recognized that his elder son had special intellectual gifts. He devoted long hours tutoring him from a very young age in English, math, and the workings of the Postal Service. One year (probably late 1917 or early 1918) when Shi-Chao was ill with scarlet fever and reportedly on the brink of death, Enlin took over the responsibilities of his father's Postmaster position. He ran the whole operation for nearly two months while his father lay immobilized—and he was only twelve years old.

(It was likely that Enlin's father actually had the pandemic influenza i.e., the Spanish flu which was rampant in 1918, and which was commonly misdiagnosed as scarlet fever since scarlet fever itself was quite rare at that time.)

Enlin Pan (Emma's husband, 1905-1978)

Enlin was born in Fu-Yang, Chekiang Province (known for being the center of the paper industry). Because his father was assigned to various posts throughout the province, the Pan family moved quite often while maintaining the family home in Hangzhou. Enrolled in various schools while simultaneously being tutored by his father accelerated Enlin's education to where he surpassed his elder sister by age five. He completed algebra and English at seven and attended the University of Shanghai at 14 earning his BS in Chemistry at 17 in 1922.

Enlin excelled in speech and music, which led him to become chief debater for intercollegiate debate competitions as well as the university symphony conductor and singer. He developed considerable proficiency in the English language structure, which later culminated in publishing textbooks on the subject. He held several academic positions including professor of English at Northeastern University, University of Shanghai, and the University of Chekiang, plus Mathematics at the American School.

Enlin left the academic world to become the Chinese Deputy Postmaster General. After serving in that post a short time, he concluded the post was too political and left to join Shanghai Commercial Bank as a Foreign Exchange and Personnel Manager, as well as one of its Directors. Simultaneously, he wrote the only foreign exchange text book for college use at the time. A few years later, he added the prestigious position as President of the China Travel Service to his long list of accomplishments.

1932
Enlin's Mother (Soong Tsu Tsen)

1942
Enlin's Father (Pan Shi-Chao)

18.
ROMANTIC GETAWAY, SORT OF

In the late 1930s and early 1940s, the Japanese army gradually pushed the Chinese forces westward. As a result, the Chinese government also had to constantly migrate westward and reestablish their functionality. To help facilitate this task, the government relied heavily on an advance guard of experts to arrange and procure housing for their core military command and critical civil servants.

The Chinese government approached the China Travel Service to assist them in this effort, as it was the only organization with the expertise, personnel, and in-depth resources to take on such an immense task. As President of the China Travel Service, Enlin was volunteered by the parent company, Shanghai Commercial Bank, to aid the Chinese government in this effort for a small token fee per year.

Enlin spent more and more time on the road supporting the war effort and less time courting Emma. He was about to set out on yet another such trip. As this particular venture was to scout hotels in a relatively remote, low risk region of the country, not yet threatened by the Japanese incursion, he decided it would be safe for Emma to accompany him—if she so wished.

"I have another trip coming up next week. Would you care to join me this time? I need to check some hotels in the west to make sure they're suitable for the government's needs. I have received clearance from my superiors to bring you along as a guest—if you so wish?"

"Of course, I would!" enthused Emma.

"I must warn you, the region we'll be traveling to is quite primitive, so we won't be enjoying many luxuries. If you'd like to change your mind, I'll understand."

"Where you go, I go."

So, it was arranged.

Emma hated to be separated from the love of her life for long periods of time; given the opportunity to join him, she jumped at the chance without a second thought. However, she romanticized a trip rather different than the one she had actually signed up for. An oversight—Enlin neglected to mention some of the more arduous details.

Emma packed a few nice clothes in a small suitcase (she was warned to travel light) and was waiting when his car arrived the morning of their departure. All was fine until the third day when they ran out of paved roads. Two days later, the well-maintained dirt roads degenerated to poorly maintained, badly rutted roads, then trails, and finally primitive paths. From that point on, each was carried in a rattan chair by four porters over paths that were difficult to negotiate even for the carriers. An additional set of porters followed with their luggage.

The hotels in the beginning of their journey soon gave way to small quaint inns, which then became more rustic guesthouses. Eventually these too dropped until they were sleeping on straw beds in barns. Emma managed to purchase a few basic clothing items while passing through the guesthouse phase of their accommodations and relegated her fancier garments to a permanent home at the bottom of her suitcase for the remainder of their trip. Although this was not the romantic getaway Emma had envisioned, the lovebirds cherished every moment of it—adventure and hardship included, as long as they were together. The things people do for love.

19.
FOREIGN GUESTS ONLY

On one foray, Mr. Pan reached a pre-war tourist city, much of which would soon be occupied by government officials as the Chinese government bureaucracy relocated southwestward ahead of the advancing Japanese. Upon his arrival at the finest hotel in town, he approached the desk and inquired about the availability of a room.

"I'm sorry sir, but it is Madam's policy not to rent rooms to Chinese—foreign guests only."

That seems unusual, Enlin thought, so he inquired further. "And can you tell me why this is her policy?"

"The local Chinese are disrespectful of the furnishings and tend to trash the place. They think nothing of resting muddy boots on a fine antique upholstered chair, pocketing various accouterments such as serving spoons, or even worse, lighting a fire in their rooms to cook a freshly plucked chicken," was the manager's unapologetic reply.

Mr. Pan, understanding that this city was rather rural and lacked sophistication, withdrew without complaint and found a lesser quality hotel nearby. He returned, however, to the first hotel later that evening to dine—Madam did not restrict Chinese from dining in her hotel, particularly as business was so slow. Mr. Pan struck up a conversation with the head waiter in the nearly abandoned dining room and by dessert they were on cordial terms.

"Who is this Madam you speak so much of? Is she the proprietor or just the hotel manager?"

"She is a refined Portuguese lady who inherited the hotel from her father a few years ago when it was in its heyday. She's not been happy of late because business has dwindled considerably since the beginning of the Japanese invasion. All she really wants is to retire back in Portugal, her homeland."

"She must be looking to sell then?"

"She hasn't exactly expressed those sentiments in so many words but has at times hinted that she wished to unburden herself."

"Is she in the hotel at this moment?"

"Why, yes. I believe I saw her enter her office a few minutes ago."

"Here is my card. Please present it to her and inform her that Mr. Enlin Pan wishes to speak with her."

And with a noticeably more attentive and respectful "Yes, sir," the waiter left the room only to return a few minutes later.

"She'll spare you ten minutes, but I must warn you, she is a tough lady and is in an especially foul mood."

Mr. Pan found her office door ajar. Before he could knock or even exchange pleasantries, she snapped, "What do you want? I'm a very busy woman so don't waste my time."

Given such a brisk and rude response to his presence, Enlin came straight to the point. "I have been led to believe that you wish to return to Portugal and would consider selling your hotel—if you could get a decent price for it."

"Who told you that? Never mind, doesn't matter. Yes, it's true. But what's it to you? You're obviously a stranger in these parts—you wouldn't understand the local market. You wouldn't last a week running this hotel. And besides, I will accept only escudos or gold—no Chinese money; it's worthless."

"And what do you consider to be a fair price?"

"My hotel is worth at least 60,000 escudos but under the circumstances, I might accept 40,000. There's no way someone like you could come up with that kind of cash anyhow. Now, please leave—I have much to do."

"Madam, please indulge me just a bit longer. Who is your banker?"

"Mr. Chou at the Bank of China. Why?"

"Ring him up and tell him Mr. Pan of the China Travel Service is in your office and wishes to buy your hotel for 40,000 escudos."

"Tomorrow, I'll call tomorrow—it's too late now."

"No," Mr. Pan insisted. He picked up the handset and handed it to her. "You see, Madam, I too am very busy. Call him at home now or not at all."

The sudden authoritarian firmness in this man's voice took her by surprise. A bit stunned, she took the phone from him and made the call with no further objections. A sleepy voice answered: "Hello? Hello, who is this? Do you realize what time it is? Call back in the morning."

"Wait, Mr. Chou. This is Madam Picado. Mr. Chou, I am sorry to disturb you at this late hour, but there is a crackpot in my office who claims he can buy my hotel for 40,000 escudos—he won't leave until I at least check with you."

"Good grief, have him see me in the morning. Who is this crackpot anyway?"

"Says his name is Enlin Pan from the China Travel Service."

"Oh, oh my! Mr. Pan! Is he in town? Oh, goodness. Why didn't you say so? I had no idea he was here. Mr. Enlin Pan? Think of that. That's totally different. No problem. No problem at all. I can have the money for you first thing in the morning if Mr. Pan is the buyer. Would 10:30 be okay, Madam Picado?" And not waiting for an answer, he hung up.

She stared openmouthed, first at the dead phone, then at Mr. Pan as she slowly returned the handset to its cradle—almost in a trance. He acknowledged her awe with a barely perceptible nod and took his leave. "See you at the bank then, 10:30?"

He then approached the front desk, only to be greeted once again by the desk clerk's disclaimer, "I really am sorry sir. But as I mentioned before, Chinese are not permitted to stay here. You understand." Then the clerk busied himself with shuffling papers signaling that his conversation with Mr. Pan was over. Mr. Pan had been dismissed.

Enlin waited about fifteen seconds without moving to enhance the impact of what he was about to do. The clerk, annoyed by the Chinese man's continued presence, returned his attention and was about to dismiss him in a more forceful manner (and embarrass himself beyond repair,) when Enlin took charge.

"And what is your name?"

"Juan, Juan Perez. But..."

"Well, Juan Perez, listen carefully," Enlin continued in a slow assertive voice. "For I am not used to repeating myself. I will be returning tomorrow around noon, by which time I want the entire top floor vacated. You can give guests staying there two days' rent credit for their inconvenience but, if they wish to remain in this hotel, they must relocate to the lower floors. I will be moving into the entire top floor so make sure it is ready for me by four."

"But..."

"Also, you may inform the staff that as of noon tomorrow, I am the new owner."

Juan Perez, with mouth totally agape, shifted his gaze to Madam Picado who had just come up behind Enlin.

"It is true, Juan," she confirmed. "Mr. Pan is now your new boss."

Enlin continued, "I want you to assemble the entire staff in the main lobby early afternoon, say two-thirty, so I can address them all in person. Furthermore, tell them to not worry about their jobs; if they are in good standing, they will be retained with a five percent increase in their salary."

And before the desk clerk could recover, Mr. Pan said, "Good night Mr. Perez" and departed.

20.
MR. PAN MUST REPORT!

The fall of 1941 was approaching, and Enlin felt things were getting far too dicey for him and his family—even in the supposedly neutral Shanghai International Zone.

It had been his routine to pick up Emma in his company-chauffeured car and stop by their favorite hole-in-the-wall noodle stand to enjoy a modest lunch together each day. The lovebirds (that's how they still called themselves some thirty years later) wanted to spend as much time together as possible, especially in such uncertain times. Love does not take a vacation. However, as the political situation continued to deteriorate, they felt it prudent to adopt lower profile routines and abandon their lunch forays. Enlin thereafter brought his lunch to his office while Emma did the same.

One day Enlin sat alone eating his lunch in the corner of his outer office with his coat draped over the back of his chair, tie loosened, and collar unbuttoned. Casually dressed, he sported the demeanor of a low-level office assistant during his downtime. He purposely avoided betraying the authority he normally would command—a trait that, as it turned out, served him well.

Suddenly, without even the pretense of a courtesy knock, the door opened unceremoniously, and three Japanese officers barged in. The Major, spotting only the lone *clerk* in the office, looked disappointed but approached him anyway and demanded, "Where is Mr. Pan? I demand to see Mr. Pan immediately!"

Quickly assessing the situation, Enlin lowered his head in feigned respect and responded in a subservient voice, "Sir, Mr. Pan just left for lunch, then I believe he plans to attend some official bank meetings. He should be back around four. Is there any way I may be of service?"

"Certainly not. Give this letter to Mr. Pan when he returns. Tell him he is hereby ordered to report to Colonel Yamaguchi immediately."

"Oh, yes sir. I'll be sure he receives the message the moment he returns."

"Be sure you do, or it will go very hard on you!"

The soldiers turned and departed as abruptly as they had arrived, slamming the door behind them to confirm they were very important and not to be messed with.

So pompous, Enlin thought. He grabbed his coat and a small bag he kept in his office closet just in case such an event should occur, and inconspicuously left his office by an alternate route. He knew it was too risky to return to his quarters, plus he no longer kept anything of value there. Instead, he headed straight to his contacts at the docks. Two hours later, after sending Emma a pre-agreed encrypted message confirming his intentions, he boarded a small freighter and sailed out of the harbor and made his way to Singapore. It was a week later, when the Japanese seized control of the Shanghai International Zone, that Emma emulated his example and pursued her own exodus plans across the expansive Japanese-occupied China towards the Chinese free zone.

As he left Shanghai, Enlin finally read the letter delivered by the visiting Japanese officers. He learned his suspicions about the Japanese officers' visit were correct. The Japanese Colonel's objective was to "invite" Mr. Pan to head the Ministry of Communication in their puppet government in Nanjing (Nanking)—an invitation where refusal was not an option.

After his hasty departure from Shanghai in 1941, Mr. Pan planned to work for a few weeks in Singapore, the 278 sq. mile British naval base colony island off the southern tip of Malaysia, then make a short visit to the Philippines—all under the auspices of the China Travel Service and as a Managing Director of the Shanghai Commercial Bank.

While housed in the Raffles Hotel in Singapore shortly after 4 am on the morning of Dec 8th, 1941 (Dec 7th in Hawaii), Enlin was awakened by a cacophony of diving aircraft, gunfire, and loud explosions—Japan had launched a multiple surprise attack against all its Major Asian Pacific adversaries, including the British fleet in Singapore.

The British colonial government assured all residents that Singapore was well defended by its nearly complete ring of guns facing out to sea. However, they had made a serious oversight. Instead of attacking from the sea, the Japanese did the unexpected—they initiated their attack north of Singapore and quickly fought their way down the Malay Peninsula. Not expecting a threat from the north, the British had deployed neither adequate artillery nor sufficient troops to defend against an invasion from this direction. The Japanese encountered little resistance during their initial attack, especially as the Malays' relationship with the British was at an all-time low, and the people had no motivation to resist the Japanese forces just to defend the British. The Japanese rapidly moved down the Peninsula (largely on requisitioned Malaysian bicycles) and in short order attacked across the forty-mile long and one to three-mile wide Straits of Johor separating Singapore Island from Malaysia.

The British were unable to prevent the Japanese from seizing Singapore. On February 15th, seventy days after the initial attack, Singapore surrendered. The fall of Singapore is often considered one of the worst defeats the British Army has ever suffered.

Enlin was ensconced in the Raffles Hotel from day one of the attack. Once it was clear, however, that defeat was inevitable, the Chinese Consul General approached the British commanding officer and implored that he quickly evacuate Mr. Pan at all costs, as Mr. Pan played a paramount role in the war effort. His arguments swayed the commander, and Enlin was on the last flight off the island before Singapore fell.

Enlin landed in Hong Kong and was scheduled to leave for Manila in the Philippines the following day, where he planned to stay at the home of the Chinese ambassador. Bad weather grounded his flight, which set him back an additional day. That night, while Enlin waited in Hong Kong, the ambassador's residence was leveled by an intensive Japanese bombardment. The Chinese ambassador and his entire staff were killed. Enlin's guardian angel had once again intervened. Eventually Enlin returned to Chongqing where he met Emma after her terrible journey and preceded her to India and then the U.S. by ship.

1944
Enlin Pan on Newsweek Cover

Wartime Town Feb. 11, 1945

Bride Flies Perilous Route From China For Marriage Here

By Marion McEniry
Women's Editor, The Examiner

IN SAN FRANCISCO this week is a charming Chinese couple we may hear more of in the postwar world.

They are Mr. and Mrs. E. L. Pan—but only recently so.

Three weeks ago, Miss Emma Liu of Chungking landed in San Pedro, Calif.; telephoned Mr. Pan, head of the China Travel Service, then on business in New York. They met in San Francisco, were married at the First Congregational Church, and are honeymooning at the St. Francis.

That San Francisco meeting was the last lap of a prenuptial trip extraordinary even in these days. To reach her bridegroom-elect, Miss Liu had made the hazardous flight "over the hump" to India and thence to the United States—an experience still somewhat rare for women.

When we asked tiny, reed-slim Mrs. Pan—beautiful and fragile looking in her turquoise Chinese gown—if she feared her flight over the world's highest mountains, she said quickly, "Not at all. It was—what you call—smooth. A wonderful American pilot. Chinese co-pilot. Very secure."

"It's just a routine trip now," her husband put in. "Those boys have flown the hump so often they know it as a motorist knows a familiar road." ... So another illusion of high hazard is shattered. Or is it? Mr. Pan, after all, is in the travel business.

1945

San Francisco Chronicle Announcement Feb. 11, 1945

Jan. 20, 1945

1945
Emma and Enlin Wedding Picture

1945
Emma and Enlin at Niagara Falls

21.
TOGETHER AT LAST

After Enlin escaped from Shanghai to Singapore, then Hong Kong, he finally managed to reach Chongqing (Chungking), the war capital of Free China. Once there, he tapped into the vast Chinese intelligence networks to follow Emma's progress as she wended her way westward. Emma and her little band fled Shanghai and zigzagged as unobtrusively as possible across occupied China. They used any form of transportation they could muster including by foot, bus, and crammed into the rear of open-backed trucks. When on foot, they took turns carrying Emma's elderly mother on their backs, as her bound feet hindered her progress.

Once Emma's small band finally reached Free China, Enlin was able to extend his long guardian-angel arm to see to it that she and her companions were properly taken care of. He found Emma's mother (who was in poor health at the time) and sister (who was taking care of their mother) a small apartment owned by the China Travel Service in Guilin. Emma continued to Chongqing where she found work and was able to remit funds to her mother and sister for support. It was here that the lovebirds reunited and were together whenever Enlin was not off on important government business for the war effort, until he departed China for the U.S. in early 1943. They would not meet again until January 5th, 1945, almost two years after their separation.

One night, tired of hiding out during Japanese bombing raids, Enlin and Emma sat calmly atop a bunker holding hands—and talked. They pledged their love for each other and decided that once the war was over, they wanted to have children and to raise them in an environment of freedom, even if it meant they had to leave behind their possessions, their families, and their homeland.

Enlin's work took him to many places during this period, including long stretches in India. During one such long trip, he received instructions to represent the Shanghai Commercial Bank at an international conference in New York. The lovebirds seized upon this opportunity to plan a life together that would begin in America. As part of this plan, Enlin pulled off the virtually impossible task, while in India, of securing a coveted seat for Emma on a flight "over the hump," out of China in late 1944.

After a circuitous path winning a China-wide competitive scholarship to study abroad, Emma arrived in San Pedro, California where Enlin met her as she disembarked the ship. They traveled up the coast and shortly after their arrival, were married in San Francisco January 20th, 1945. They checked into the St. Francis Hotel next door on Union Square for their all-too-short honeymoon, before pressing matters required Enlin's return to New York.

Enlin and Emma were initially housed by his company at the luxurious Mayflower Hotel on Madison Avenue in New York, where their first daughter, Chiahua, was born (nearly nine months later to the day). They next moved into a nearby penthouse apartment with a private elevator at 55 Madison Avenue and hired a nanny. They enjoyed their upper-class lifestyle in New York City during that period—an unusually luxurious lifestyle considering the U.S. was at war. Unfortunately, Emma did not enjoy all the amenities of her station as much as one might expect, since domestic help was difficult to come by and her cooking skills were near zero. Numerous visitors passing through stayed with them as the bank's guests during this time. Emma, who as a child grew up in a home with thirty some servants, did her best to fill the roles of cooking and cleaning, as well as hostess.

After the war's end, Enlin retained his Executive Vice President position with his bank in New York. There, he was able to hire a housecleaner, a private cook, and a nanny for their first two children. His reputation as an astute international businessman had grown considerably.

All that changed when the Communists prevailed in their struggle to seize power from the Nationalists on December 7th, 1949. They further consolidated their hold on Mainland China when they successfully deflected the Nationalists' reinvasion attempt from Taiwan on March 18th, 100 days later. There was great excitement in some of the local New York Chinese communities, as many idealists felt that Chiang Kai-Shek's regime was far too corrupt. They speculated that the Communists, reputedly less corrupt, had a better chance to begin a clean slate and rebuild a more prosperous post-war China.

The Pans were suspicious of the intentions and level of corruption in both regimes and were reticent to join the bandwagon of those patriotic overseas Chinese who wished to return to Communist China to embrace the New China.

They conferred with several of their friends who had chosen to return. As a precaution, the friends had agreed to embed a word sequence in their letters, to inform the Pans whether it was prudent for them to follow. They suspected that letters leaving China would be intercepted, forged, or censored, so they relied on the code to convey the real state of affairs.

Letters written during the first few months by their friends following their return to China were surprisingly positive, and they assured the Pans that they had made the right decision. But then the tone changed abruptly and, although the text strongly praised the regime and begged the Pans to join them, the hidden encryptions warned, "Don't come! All is not well here." These were followed shortly after with, "Very dangerous—they lied to us." By the sixth month these letters from China did not even appear to be in their friends' own hand and began to solicit money due to personal financial hardship.

The Pans purposely broke off all contact with their friends thereafter. They figured a total communication break was the best course of action for all involved. This proved to be prudent. At the height of the Cultural Revolution, anyone who had even the slightest ties abroad was considered an enemy of the state; they were subject to extra severe treatment, and were sentenced to long hours of back-breaking work in the fields, forced to endure arduous self-criticism sessions, or even sent to prison.

The family letters and photographs did, in fact, create hardship for several family members (and in a few cases, prison), even though the Pans were extra cautious to assure the content was neutral—mostly about health and progress of young children. Possessing photographs of relatives in America was enough to brand a person as suspect.

During this transition period, both the Communist and the Nationalist governments solicited Enlin to return (to Beijing on the one hand and Taipei on the other) and accept the prominent role of foreign minister. Simultaneously, other parts of the two governments extended offers for Enlin to become the "true" president of the former Shanghai Commercial Bank. Both the Nationalists and the Communists claimed control of the bank.

The Pans concluded that neither government was free from corruption and all options of their returning to Asia were too risky, especially with their now three young children. With all the turmoil in the two Chinas, his bank closed its U.S. office, and Enlin found himself out of a job, his Chinese assets unretrievable. China closed behind them.

This high-class couple's situation now morphed into a struggling unemployed, postwar immigrant family. They explored various options, including an import/export business of their own, but lost most of their remaining nest egg to an unscrupulous partner. Eventually, Enlin accepted a position with an established import/export company in the family-friendly city of Cincinnati, Ohio.

When she and the three children joined Enlin by train from New York to their new home, Emma became depressed. She cried for a year trying to figure out, "What is this place, Ohio?"

22.
THE COMMUNISTS TAKE OVER

–

1949

Soon after the Communist takeover, Chinese expats in the U.S. began to receive real estate tax bills against their Chinese property, to which they still held title. As the bills seemed reasonable at first, most of the expats complied and paid them. A year later the real estate taxes doubled, then doubled again. Many people continued to pay these taxes, at least during the first few years, hoping to retain ownership of their property—except for Enlin and Emma. By this time, relations between the U.S. and China had deteriorated drastically, and Enlin saw the writing on the wall. Instead of paying taxes that doubled each year until they became unpayable, giving the government an excuse to confiscate the property, Enlin and Emma donated their property to the government with a letter commending their leadership. This action kept the Pans off the *persona non grata* blacklist of people who were not allowed to enter China or even do business there. Their action proved quite useful to my wife and myself many years later when we visited China during the summer of 1979.

Most of the Pan and Liu relatives left behind in China suffered significant hardship, due to their previous aristocratic status and education as well as their family connections abroad. All Chinese with overseas relatives were suspect. All communication was censored and often resulted in some form of punishment. At the same time, the Chinese who remained were instructed that it was their patriotic duty to solicit money from all overseas family members. Most relatives who remained were sent to the countryside to be reeducated, especially the scholars and anyone considered to be middle-class or above.

Emma and Enlin would regularly remit small amounts of money as well as clothing packages to their relatives, large enough to help but not so much as to draw attention or complicate their lives. The Pans did encourage their three young children to send small sums to the elders as well (particularly their grandparents) with short notes written in their own hand. The children earned the money, their notes explained, by doing chores and odd jobs for neighbors. As these amounts were small and came from grandchildren, they brought no government reprisal. The Communists still held elders in high regard. Only many years later did the grandchildren learn that their remittances had brought considerable happiness to these elders and while small, were significant to improving their living situations.

Thirty Years Later

My wife and I delayed our honeymoon until the summer of 1979, just after she graduated from Stanford Business School. We planned a relatively modest (i.e., graduate student honeymoon budget) Around-the-World trip in 80 Days on Pan American at their special fare of $1,199 each. We each carried one of two small shared backpacks. The first contained our few clothes and toiletries while the second served two purposes: on the way out, it contained gifts for relatives in China, while returning home, these gifts were replaced by gifts for friends and stateside relatives.

Traveling in China as tourists in 1979 was still very rare (China barely opened to the west in 1972 with Nixon's visit) so both we (the tourists) and they (the China Travel Service) were unsure how it all worked. We further complicated our logistics as we traveled with no itinerary and no guides—unheard of at the time. We did obtain visas in San Francisco before we began our travels, but they were issued for only three cities in China and did not include many of the destinations we wished to visit. While in Hong Kong, we visited the official China Travel Service office to seek additional visas, a day before we were to catch our train for Guangzhou (Canton).

Our initial request was denied: "Tourists are only authorized to visit three cities."

"We'd like to see your Director please, if he is in."

"You're in luck. He just returned from a meeting, and might be able to see you now."

After tea was brought in, we asked the head man if we could have visas for more than three cities. He parroted the clerk's previous response that three was the limit. After teacup refills two, three, four, and five, small talk finally led to the Director's question, "Why do you wish to visit so many cities?" Meimei answered, "My father left Shanghai in 1943 after devoting several years to resisting the Japanese incursion, and we want to visit some of those places where he and our family lived."

"Oh, that's interesting. And in what form did his resistance take place?"

"He was the President of the China Travel Service."

"What?" The man sat up straight and broke into a giant smile. "I see your name is Pan. Was your father by any chance Enlin Pan?"

"Why, yes."

At which point his deputy entered with tea, round six.

"Miss Wong, I want you to meet Mrs. Raehua Pan and her husband, Mr. Lynn Jacobson. Mrs. Pan's father was President of the China Travel Service forty years ago. By the way, why have we limited their visa to three cities?"

"That's all they need."

"Is there a rule that actually limits them to three destinations?"

"No."

"Then give them as many as they want."

Miss Wong seemed taken aback but immediately replied, "Yes sir," took our passports and our list of the additional cities we hoped to visit and left the room.

Her boss swung his attention back to Meimei and explained his reactions, "When I was just a teenage office boy, your father was my boss and mentor. I worshiped him. He was so kind and patient—not like the other managers who treated us low level workers so poorly. I learned so much from him—almost like going to my own form of business school. He recognized my abilities and gave me my first chance to learn the trade.

"I've never forgotten him and am only too happy, in some small way, that I can make it up to him through his daughter and son-in-law."

After tea rounds seven and eight (it seemed like fifty), Miss Wong returned with our processed passports, handed them to us, whispered into her boss's ear, and left the room.

"Miss Wong just informed me that a search on your father's file showed he was not an enemy of the state and in fact is still held in the highest possible regard—making your unlimited travel possible."

Finally, halfway through teacup nine, my near-exploding bladder dictated we thank our benefactor for his most gracious assistance, avail ourselves of their restrooms, and take our leave.

Dinner with Engineers

A week later our relatives in Beijing made elaborate arrangements for us to have dinner at a local restaurant with them and three engineers from their company; it proved most interesting. Again, if Enlin had been on the bad list, this dinner would never have been possible. The engineers were well past normal retirement age and in fact, had been pulled out of retirement to help their country reclaim some of its technical expertise. They spoke quite earnestly but kept their voices low for waiters were often frontline government spies.

"Are you having difficulty getting new graduates then?" I asked surprisedly, after learning that their retirement had been suspended.

"No, far from it. But that's most of the problem, not the solution."

"How so?"

"During the Cultural Revolution (1969 to 1979), academic promotion had been based on how well students could cite Mao's Little Red Book and not on merit, that is, not on their ability to master course material. They were encouraged to mock and humiliate their professors. Many academicians, made to confess imaginary errors, were either removed from teaching, left the teaching profession on their own, or greatly dumbed down their material to placate their unprepared, overconfident students. As a result, any engineers we have in our department under twenty-five are totally inept."

"What do you do about them then?"

"That's why we've been pulled out of retirement. We may be a bit out of date, but we're still light years ahead of the recent graduates."

"Yes," broke in a second engineer. "We tell them that they will still get paid, but at the same time ask them to sit in the corner and stay out of the way."

Meeting People on the Street

During this extraordinary visit to China, we met many people who had known Mr. Pan from the pre-Communist era—all spoke of him with the greatest respect. We met a gardener (who used to shine Mr. Pan's shoes) at Suzhou (Souchou) University, where Mr. Pan taught Chemistry and English; he considered Mr. Pan "one of the good ones." Many dignitaries and scholars appeared at our hotel to pay their respects. Once word got out about our visit, relatives hundreds of miles away received time off to visit us. One couple was given new housing, while others received promotions and substantial raises, even though we didn't visit their cities.

At the same time, waiters, cab drivers, and service people (all agents) kept an eye on us. At one hotel I threw a badly ripped T-shirt into a wastebasket with no second thought. When we arrived to check in at our next city, there it was. Not only neatly folded on the bed, but it had been washed and mended. At each city, we could see our suitcases had been gone through and rearranged. Papers were shuffled.

One day we rented bikes and rode around Beijing. As we passed other bikers, Meimei greeted them with a smile, a nod of her head, and a friendly "Ni hao!"

"Meimei, you have to stop being so friendly."

"Why?"

"Look behind you."

She stopped and looked back, "Oh."

Behind us was a trail of young men and their crashed bicycles. Even though Meimei was wearing a modest full-length dress, it was sleeveless (temperature 95 degrees), which was considered very risqué in China in 1979. Her relatives constantly tried to put sweaters over her bare shoulders and eventually sewed her a more modest dress which she wore.

What my wife and I witnessed at the very opening of China under the Communist regime was quite extraordinary. It was a third world country undergoing an almost violent transition. We were fortunate to visit China multiple times since then and observed the huge metamorphosis on each subsequent visit as restrictions were loosened, people began to participate in entrepreneurship, and took more control of their own prosperity. China has evolved into a world power and player.

1971
Enlin at 66 After Heart Attack

**ALLAN HENRY JACOBSON
AND
CHARLOTTE GRANT JACOBSON,**
AUTHOR'S PARENTS

1904
The Three Orphaned Grant Sisters: Author's mother,
Charlotte Jacobson (on left), Margo Black, and Nell West

1950
Allan Showing Off his 33' Owens Cabin Cruiser
St. Albans Bay, Lake Minnetonka

1963
Catch of the Day (Allan Jacobson squatting on left)
Pompano Beach, Florida

23.

THEM

We know very little about THEM, about their history that is, before WE came into the picture. By THEM, I mean both our father, Allan Henry Jacobson (December 19, 1895-1971), and our mother Charlotte Grant (September 12, 1898-1982). By WE, I mean Richard, my three-year older brother and myself—both adopted in the 1930s.

As I sifted through my mother's papers after her death, I found very little material that addressed their early histories. My mother outlasted my father by eleven years, over which time perhaps, she purged references to their histories while downsizing from a large home on Lake Minnetonka (15 miles west of Minneapolis), to a medium-sized apartment, a small apartment, and finally to an assisted living facility in Bloomington. Keeping documents through all those transitions may simply have been too much of a burden, or maybe it would have exposed past life events she did not wish to reveal. In any event, very few records remained, so I had to draw on the rare verbal tidbits dropped on me by THEM from time to time.

One surprising sentence my mother uttered on her death bed with a tear in her eye, was "I loved her so much." Could this have been a reference to an abortion, a daughter she lost or given up for adoption, her mother or even a favorite sister?

Neither my mother nor father had normal upbringings. Both my mother's parents died when she was very young. She was placed at five years old in an all-girls Catholic boarding school with her two older sisters, seven-year-old Nell Grant (West) and nine-year-old Margo Grant (Black), where they were heavily indoctrinated by strict nuns through high school.

My mother had a deprived upbringing, but not in a financial sense. Deprivation came from a lack of family love, support, and normal family interactions. When her parents died (the cause never revealed), her adult relatives swooped in and appropriated all the family's worldly goods of value (furniture, tools, and kitchenware) with the justification that children so young had no need for such things. By the time the three of them became aware of how much the relatives had absconded, most of them had disappeared. I never saw a single photo of a relative other than her sisters, and am aware of only one phone call, from a cousin, when I was six.

Her parents, a schoolteacher and an engineer, had been better off than the average middle class family, so funds available from the will were sufficient to send all three girls to boarding school. The judge handling the case appointed himself trustee of the estate. It seems he found it convenient (as reported by my mother) to double bill the trust for the three sisters' school expenses, draining the trust to his own advantage—while leaving just enough funds for my mother to complete two years of Catholic college.

The judge's wife had no affinity for children and after hosting them during their first school vacation, banned them from further household visits. The Judge's solution? Put the girls up in a local hotel during school vacations where he could arrange for their meals, pay someone to see they were clothed and provided for, and send them back to boarding school when vacations were over.

The only information I have from my mother about her boarding school experiences are:

1) She took German and remembered only a half-dozen words.

2) As the youngest, she was always left with the least desirable piece of chicken at Sunday dinners ("the pope's nose" or "the part that flew over the fence last".)

3) Her older sisters provided her some protection from being bullied at school.

4) She and her sisters' most severe punishable transgression was taking a photograph of themselves pretending to smoke with candy cigarettes.

My father had a different family situation. His father, the manager of the local lumber yard, died suddenly (details unknown) in 1909 when my father was fourteen. His mother, a widow with three kids, Allan, Eddie, and Beatrice, remarried shortly thereafter and took on the name of Peterson. This new situation left Allan rudderless, and he dropped out of school after eighth grade. He only made it that far because he doubled up on shop (he loved wood-working tools.)

My father was not happy with his new stepfather or home situation. He couldn't wait to get out of his stifling hometown, Swea City, Iowa, population just over 400, with its limited opportunities. He was more than ready to start his own life's story. His chance came when his charismatic uncle showed up for a short visit in 1911 and announced he was off to homestead in Alberta, Canada. "They have free land just for the taking! All you have to do is be eighteen and willing to work it for two years," he enthused. "Just think—forty acres! Free! And don't worry now about the eighteen-bit, I'm told they never bother to check. They just want hard working folks like you and me to help make their province thrive—they need good people!

"Got the news two days ago—want to get there before it's all taken. Figure I got at least a week's head start over all dem East Coast fellers."

That was all my father needed to hear. Two hours later, after begging his mother to let him join his uncle on the trek to Alberta, it was decided. Twenty minutes to pack a small bag the next morning, and they were gone, gone on the adventure of a lifetime. Allan thought to himself, "Ready or not world, here I come!" He had no idea what was in store for him and how ill-equipped he was at sixteen for such an adventure, having no farming experience and only the few dollars his mother slipped him at his departure. But it didn't matter. His stepfather, who considered him a bit of a burden, was not at all unhappy to see him gone. His sister and brother saw him off, but as they had never been out of Swea City themselves, couldn't comprehend how big the country was and how really far away their older brother was headed. Shortly after arriving in Alberta, reality set in. He took one look at the sod houses new homesteaders were living in and continued to Edmonton, Canada where he got a job as a bellhop. He married, divorced, and eventually migrated back to Minneapolis where he became a salesman.

My adoptive parents met in a budget resident hotel for singles where they had both taken lodging, (the shared bathroom was down the hall). My father told my mother early in their courtship that he had divorced his first wife shortly after their marriage, and she passed away soon thereafter… no details but a few made up cover stories. After his death, we received a letter from his first wife's caregiver revealing she had actually survived him by one month, and that they had casually corresponded a couple of times a year for over fifty years. Secrets, secrets, secrets!

My mother felt guilty all her life for having married a divorcee, a mortal sin in the Catholic church, and worried she might be excommunicated. The cover story of his first wife's death or that his first marriage was annulled may have been fabricated to ease her guilt.

24.
HOW THEY MET

THEY, Allan Jacobson and Charlotte Grant, met as tenants both living in the same residential, no-cooking-allowed Minneapolis singles hotel, a type popular in the early 1920s for their low cost. This generic six story residential hotel, like several of its time, consisted of rather Spartan furnished, single-rooms with shared bathrooms (and a sometimes-hot shower) down the hall. The utilitarian lobby sported a few overstuffed and tired matching chairs, a reception desk, a pay phone and a half-star café utilized mainly by residents on tight schedules and challenging budgets .

The hotel management was quite militant in enforcing their no-cooking policy due to fear of mice, objectionable odors, cockroach infestation, and most of all, fire. Most residents toed the line and either ate at the small hotel café or took their meals out. A few cut costs and ate cold food in their rooms or used clandestine hot plates. In any event, blown fuses and poor ventilation made resident cooking easy to detect.

My parents met while passing through the hotel's revolving door; their daily working hours were quite regular with overlapping schedules. The frequent lobby encounters and a shortage of unoccupied dining tables eventually led to their occasionally sharing a table during meals. After a six-month courtship, they consolidated living spaces. At the time, my father was in sales for a meat butchering equipment company, and my mother worked nearby at City Hall. They slept and dressed in my father's room and ate, socialized, and stored their overflow belongings in my mother's room. As my mother had been orphaned at five and my father's mother had since moved to Fontana, California with his sister and brother, there was no family on either side to censor cohabitation. They suppressed the fact from my brother and me that shortly after they started dating, they had merged their living situations. I'm sure a great many of their activities (they partied a lot) also went unreported to support a high moral image they wished to project, a standard deception of parents in all eras. Pet nicknames for each other, Jakie and Charlie, also disappeared a few years later after we came along, perhaps to further promote an image of respectability.

My parents' financial situation improved considerably in the early 1930s, which enabled them to buy a home at 4717 11th Ave South in a newly developed Minneapolis neighborhood, where they attempted to start a family. After a couple of years of no-go, they decided to adopt, first Richard Louis from Minneapolis in 1935 and then myself, Lynn Allan from Spokane in 1938. I had been relocated by the Salvation Army Home for Unwed Mothers in Spokane to Minneapolis at only a few months old, however my actual placement with the Jacobsons was delayed for several months as the agency thought I had a serious asthma condition which turned out to be just a bad cold. I was finally officially placed with my adopting parents a little before my first birthday. The final birth certificate didn't catch up, however, until I was in graduate school. My father's sister, Beatrice, was also unable to get pregnant while both my mother's sisters had two children each, so the infertility most likely stemmed from his side of the family.

My father did very well in the automobile business during and after WWII, to the point we were able to move up and purchase a large rustic stone home with 500 feet of shoreline on Lake Minnetonka's St Albans Bay, fifteen miles west of Minneapolis. It was a matter of being in the right place at the right time and taking the initiative to make something of it. From third grade to college graduation, that was my home.

1947
Allan & Charlotte Jacobson taking a dip
in Lake Minnetonka (St. Albans Bay)
in front of our Minnesota home

25.
ADOPTION

Neither my mother nor father had any idea how to raise children. Directions were not yet in their playbook. WE were raised by parents who did the best THEY could, but my father worked fourteen hours a day, seven days a week trying to build his business, and my mother was absorbed in her gardening, housework, and learning to cook while trying to maintain a semblance of social life with two rambunctious boys. Things didn't always go smoothly. A crescendo of family arguments at the dinner table where our father often bullied my brother for not doing better in school drove me to eat dinner alone in the basement in front of a 12" grainy black and white TV. I spent most of my childhood alone. I explored our lake by canoe in the summer, tramped through the surrounding woods on foot in the fall, and traveled every abandoned dirt road within ten miles on my motor scooter, my birthday gift at age nine. This was my refuge. I became an expert at catching frogs which I sold for bait and turtles, which I gave to friends as pets, and when a bit older, water skied. My strongest recollection was that I donned a bathing suit in June, slept in it all summer, and removed it at the end of August in time for school. Since I spent eight hours a day in the lake, showers were not part of my summer routine. I spent so much time in the water that I was in danger of morphing into a giant prune.

In retrospect, I was a loner, a thinker, shy, and a bit reclusive. I was reluctant to use the phone, and though I had several casual friends, none were really close with the exception of Tom Gessner, my closest friend, whom I met during my Junior year in high school. I mostly felt like I was raising myself. Although this left me socially immature, it did allow me to concentrate on sports despite polio at fourteen (I was bedridden at Sister Kenny Hospital for six weeks.) I held the high school pole vault and college breaststroke school records. My alone thinking time also helped me achieve the all-high school mathematics award during my sophomore year. My reclusive nature made me less prone to peer pressure traps such as smoking, drinking, and hooliganism.

"Oh," she said, "we adopted two."

I was sixish when I overheard my mother explain this fact over the phone to a person from her past. I was sure she was talking about WE but had no idea what *adopted* meant. A born optimist, I assumed it was something good and stored this minor detail in a corner of my brain for future access. But when I bragged about it to Margaret, a girl in my fourth grade class, she set me straight stating in a slightly demeaning tone, "What are you bragging about? Adoption is when your real parents don't want you and give you away." This surprising and blunt rebuttal of my origin's value, for some reason, had very little impact on me at the time. When I confronted my mother with my newly acquired understanding of adoption, she responded with the clearly rehearsed pat answer, "Adopted means you're special because we got to choose you."

I can live with that, I thought, and let it drop.

Later in college, I discovered that the adoption badge affected different people in a variety of ways. Typically, when I'd meet someone else who had been adopted, we'd treat the shared experience just like new acquaintances discovering they were both from the same town in Vermont: interesting and fun only for the commonality it implied, but not much else.

Then there were people greatly affected by the 'affliction' of being adopted. When a blind date discovered that, like her, I was adopted—pow, she latched onto me like super Velcro, so much so that after two dates, I had to stop seeing her. She got attached to me so strongly that I knew the longer I waited to break up, the more difficult it would become. An overly dependent relationship would, in the long run, not be good for either one of us.

I didn't begin to search my own origins until my early sixties—at the insistence of my determined youngest daughter. My first effort was unsuccessful. I knew I was born in the Salvation Army Home for Unwed Mothers in Spokane, Washington (now an alcohol rehabilitation facility) and named Lynn Melroy Hopland at birth. Calls to the Salvation Army for information were of little help. They had my records but would not release any information to me—"Policy! You understand, don't you?"

"No, I didn't understand then and I don't understand now."

I then called all thirty-four listed Hoplands in the state of Washington, All dead ends. This process took much longer than I had anticipated as the first twenty minutes of each call was spent convincing Mr. or Ms. Hopland I was for real and not some scammer. The Hoplands, it seems, are a very suspicious group. Google was of no help with its then primitive search engine, and the Census Bureau did not release personal information less than seventy years old.

Fifteen years later my same but now even more insistent daughter, convinced me we should give it another go. So we (mostly her) tried again. Success! Census records after 70 years now revealed my mother (whose name I knew) and one of my aunts were raised in Cass Lake, MN. This led to locating an aunt's obituary, which then led to the discovery of her daughter, Trudy, on Facebook. An hour later I was talking with Trudy, my newfound cousin in Seattle. At the start of the day all my known blood relatives could sit comfortably around our dining table. By the end of the day, we would need the entire 49ers stadium to accommodate them all. But if every Hopland search call made fifteen years prior was met with total skepticism, why did my newfound cousin accept my authenticity so quickly? It turned out that she too had been put up for adoption, just after the outbreak of WWII.

Trudy's mother wrote the adoption agency many years after her adoption to request help in locating her daughter. The agency agreed to forward a contact letter to Trudy but would not provide any other information. Trudy received the letter from her mother in late April, waited a little over a week, and made the call. When the call was picked up, Trudy's first words were, "Happy Mother's Day!" They both cried for the next half hour—no words, just tears.

Following first contact, I was put in touch with several more cousins, a couple of aunts, and several next generationers. I learned my mother had been raised on a farm in Cass Lake, Mn, was the oldest of her siblings, and had me secretly (only one sister knew) while working in Bemidji, MN (15 miles to the northwest). She later became a schoolteacher and unfortunately died ten years before my second attempt to contact her. My birth father was a young man who lived on a nearby farm. She wanted to contact me but feared it would disrupt my life. She had married a widower a few years following my birth but never conceived again after having me. A couple years later with the help of a college classmate, I learned my birth father had married someone else and fathered several half siblings.

People ask, "How does this make you feel?" I do wish my birth mother had contacted me but I understand her choice. I also wish I had known my birth father, but it wasn't in the cards. It's all part of life, and so many of us live under a cloud of secrets, an array of emotional baggage, and questionable history—we endure and live the best we can without getting stuck in the past. With a happy marriage, five fabulous daughters, and a slew of grandkids making me proud, I am more involved with the future than the past. Sometimes it's okay to leave the baggage on the platform and look back with heightened compassion.

26.
CARS CARS, CARS, AND MORE CARS

—

LATE 1920s, MINNEAPOLIS, MN

"Cars, cars, cars! That's all you ever talk about, Jakie! Last night I heard you chattering in your sleep about some stunning redhead, redtop, or something like that. That got my attention. But when I put my ear up close to your mouth—turns out you were talking about a stunning red Chevy!"

Charlotte (my mother) had finally had it with my father's (her live-in boyfriend at the time) love affair with automobiles and could contain her frustration no longer. So even before her morning coffee and hotel shower down the hall, she lamented, "Cars, cars, cars! That's all you ever talk about. If it were another woman—that I could deal with—but cars? No one ever taught me how to compete with a car. This is so unfair!"

"I can't help it, Charlie," my father mumbled in defense, toothbrush in mouth. "I remember every detail of that wondrous June day in '07 when I saw my first automobile drive into town. It was love at first sight! Even though they were way too expensive for people like us to consider. They were outta reach of everyone except for Mr. Larson, the bank President, and old Mr. Anderson, the realtor, the richest two guys in Swea City, Iowa.

Two years later there were still only a handful around town. I figured I'd never be rich enough to actually get one myself, but I dreamed, I dreamed a lot. Drove a friend's car a couple times a few years later when we worked together at that hotel up in Edmonton. He was a rich college kid back for summer vacation and taught me how to drive his daddy's car—well sorta taught me. He was no great driver himself. It was wonderful though! Did I tell you about the time I first…?"

"Yes, only 500 times."

"Well, I just wanted to…"

"Look, Jakie, between your gallivanting all around town ten hours a day peddling your boring butcher supplies and spending the rest of your waking hours reading, talking, and breathing cars, I don't get enough of you. There's only one solution."

That got my father's attention. He stiffened and suddenly showed concern, "You're not thinking about breaking up with me are you!?"

"Oh, no. You're not getting off that easy. It's obvious. You have to change jobs and sell cars—simple as that. Sales is your strong point anyway. Can't imagine there's anything you don't already know about cars. Your training should take at most ten minutes, if that."

Pause—blank stare—epiphany—smile—excitement!

"By golly, Charlie, you're right! Never even occurred to me. What a great idea!"

This conversation between my father and mother marked a major turning point in their fortunes—and ultimately mine.

Between my father's newfound success selling cars (Mother was right, he was a natural) and my mother's steady income from her Hennepin County courthouse job, they were able to save a down payment for a new home in South Minneapolis, marry in 1932, adopt two sons, and acquire the obligatory dog to start the American dream. They became a basic middle-class family, and although they lacked education (eighth grade for my father and two years of a Catholic junior college with no major for my mother), they could be deemed prosperous.

27.

THE ROOKIE

–

ALLAN H. JACOBSON

Scene: Showroom of a Ford dealership in Minneapolis in the mid 1920s. The rookie salesman patiently waited his turn to greet a prospective customer when a young man, perhaps sixteen or seventeen, drifted rather tentatively into the showroom. The rookie was quite surprised when the salesman on deck, who had next-dibs-contact priority, did not rise to greet this teen as was customary—in fact none of the veteran salesmen, all at least twenty years the rookie's senior, even acknowledged his presence. It had been a slow morning, and they'd spent most of it chewing the fat; suddenly they became dreadfully busy shuffling papers and making highly animated phone calls—probably to each other.

 Mindful of sales staff protocol, the rookie of a few months waited for what he considered an appropriate length of time, and then took the initiative. He caught the eye of the next salesman in the contact queue, received a barely perceivable nod of approval, and made his move. Approaching the young man, he sported his warmest smile and outstretched his hand.

 "I can see from your expression you love cars almost as much as I do."

"Sure do," the young man responded, "Maybe more! Especially that roadster. She's a beaut!" He had clearly fallen in love. "That's the newest model, isn't it?"

"Yep! Boy, you really have an eye for cars. Just came in a few hours ago. Totally redesigned! Upgraded everything bumper to bumper —motor, clutch, transmission, suspension, even the upholstery—everything. If I could have the car of my dreams, this would be it. Awesome!

"Only been available from the factory 'bout a week. The first one we've ever had, maybe the first even in all of Minneapolis." The rookie was pretty proud of his spiel but in truth, the kid was totally hooked the moment he set eyes on it.

"We're on a quota from the company—probably won't get another one for at least a month and by then we'll have a waiting list. This powerhouse certainly won't last long—maybe not even the day."

After a considerable amount of enthusiastic back-and-forth car talk on the merits of such a fantastic vehicle, in which the two young men would finish each other's sentences, "I really want this car. I'll get my dad to come back with me around 5:30. If he agrees, then consider it sold. Can you hold it that long?"

"I can hold it 'til six, but no longer. Be unfair to hold it off the market longer than that."

"Understood. See ya then."

As the teen left, the other salesmen dropped their busy charade and turned their attention to the rookie. All chimed in:

"Boy, did you waste your time."

"Yeah, you'll never see him again."

"Listen up kid, after a few years, you'll be able to smell the tire-kickers and avoid the 'all show, no buy' types. Then you can concentrate your efforts on the real buyers and make some real money." The rookie shrugged his shoulders and answered, "I don't agree. Something about his enthusiasm, his no-bull attitude. Makes me think he's the real thing, and he'll be back—at least to check it out a second time. It's not like we're all that busy anyway."

"Dream on, kid. Trust me." The head salesman/manager turned his palms upward: "Commission? Poof! Gone. Vanished."

At that, all the old timers laughed at the naiveté of the rookie and shifted their attention on the door in the event a real customer were to show up.

Surprise! Surprise! Three hours later, the young teen returned with his father in tow. After barely five minutes, they shook the rookie's hand, wrote a check for full price with no haggling, and proudly drove their prize, the most expensive car sold that month, off the showroom floor.

The older salesmen suddenly became very subdued and busied themselves once again with shuffling papers, fetching coffee, and pretending to make important calls. The subject never came up again.

28.
FLIP SIDE OF THE COIN
–
THE VERSION WE ALL LOVE TO HEAR

Fast forward forty-five years. A young man enters an imposing Porsche showroom with the intent of fulfilling his life's dream: *Purchase a shiny, new, image-building, thill-enhancing, ultimate dream car, a Porsche sports car.* He had just returned from a high-salaried, low cost-of-living with generous per diem, tax free two year stint working on Kwajalein, a remote island in the middle of the north Pacific. His checkbook had never been so engorged and happy. Paying cash for a new Porsche would cut his liquid assets nearly in half, but at this stage in his young career, he believed the sacrifice was well worth it—he'd start saving tomorrow.

With disheveled hair, a three-day beard, wrinkled and slightly stained jeans (standard nerd attire), certainly not projecting the image of the well kept, rapidly rising, superstar lawyer type, the young man strolled onto the Porsche showroom floor and began perusing the inventory on display. He attempted to get the attention of any of the gentlemen who appeared to work there, confident he could pay cash for whatever would tickle his fancy. They all looked frightfully busy even though he seemed to be the only customer in sight. After being ignored for ten minutes, he decided to be more assertive and approached the nearest salesman. Simultaneously, a well-dressed junior executive type entered the showroom. Suddenly three salesmen appeared out of nowhere and ran over to fuss over the newcomer. Odd how so many salesmen became unbusy at the same time.

It was then that the eager, fully qualified, all-cash buyer, who had been waiting for acknowledgment from the sales staff for over twenty minutes, suddenly lost interest. He thought to himself, "Maybe I really don't need a Porsche after all." He walked out of the dealership—bank account unscathed. As he passed the last salesman on his way out, he tapped him on the shoulder and casually mentioned, "I was all set to pay cash for my dream car, but apparently you guys are much too busy to take my order." A week later, the would-be Porsche buyer refocused his financial goals from buying a status car to buying a rental house. He never got around to thanking the sales staff for ignoring him and as such, unintentionally launching him into a more prudent and profitable life-changing hobby, real estate.

An interesting note, the potential Porsche buyer was the son of the rookie salesman from 45 years earlier and this author.

29.
ONCE-A-GENERATION OPPORTUNITY

Most professional financial planners base their advice to clients on a tenuous premise: the world of assets grows steadily from decade to decade, generation to generation, and the guide for future investing is assumed to be an exponential projection of the past. Prudent financial investment planners advise their clients to invest accordingly, factoring in their age, income, retirement goals, and tolerance for risk. Their clients are advised to save regularly, diversify their specific allocations, and track them on an ongoing basis—at least often enough to avoid surprises. Sounds good.

If your planner had a crystal ball, she might foretell: "…and I can see that a major war will break out with Iceland May 18, 2027; a monster tornado will devastate eastern Montana August 27, 2029; and, of course, a major run-on gold will occur September 27, 2031, at four in the afternoon." But since crystal balls are in short supply, long-term planning tends to favor 'steady as she goes.'

It's the relatively rare anomalies that provide major opportunities—the oddly aligned confluence of circumstances whose impacts can significantly make or break our futures. But to be successful, we need the eye to see them, the courage to act upon them, and the insight to dodge scams.

In the late 1930s and early 1940s, concerns about the U.S. being dragged into another World War—fed mostly by fears rather than by facts— ran both ways.

My father thought, *We will be at war sooner than most people believe, but almost no one has acted on this prospect yet. There's an opportunity here somewhere—I can smell it.*

Cars, he thought. *Of course. People will always want their cars whether they need them or not. If hostilities expand to include the U.S., resources presently devoted to the manufacturing of cars will be diverted to the war effort. Plus, as the war continues, tires and replacement parts will become impossible to find. Conclusion, good used cars will be at a premium—and what do I do best? I sell cars!*

He thought of other items that also might be in short supply during an all-out war, but none worked for him nearly as well as cars. Cars he knew, and most other items would be too risky for him to dabble in.

He patiently began to acquire well-maintained used cars in late 1940 while they were still available and reasonably priced. He stashed them in a warehouse at a dollar per car per month. By the end of 1941, the Second World War did indeed break out. Lo and behold, as he had predicted, the supply of new cars vanished overnight, and the price of used cars soared.

Shortly thereafter, the government adopted rationing and strict price controls, which hindered his ability to further build his stockpile. By this time however, he had accumulated nearly 300 cars. He continued to operate his used car lot, but after covering his storage costs, sales were barely adequate to meet his expenses.

As a final action, my father managed to get under the rationing wire just in time to stock our attic with 500 pounds of sugar for our family's use and several master cases of cigarettes for himself, my mother, and to be used as very effective business-lubricating gifts (20 cigarettes per pack, 10 packs per carton, 50 cartons per master case make 10,000 cigarettes per master case). As he was fond of explaining to anyone who would listen some thirty years hence, accompanied with the obligatory wry smile of course, "I wanted to buy plenty of sugar and cigarettes before all those damn hoarders got 'em." For the duration of the war, we were the only kids on the block who had birthday cakes made with full recipe-strength sugar.

There are stories that during WWII, cigarettes defaulted to becoming currency in prisoner-of-war camps. Interestingly, cigarettes and silk stockings were often used as currency stateside as well, a fact not lost on my father during his negotiations with chain-smoking used car customers.

The contractor father of Stu, my graduate school roommate, saw and acted on a similar opportunity. He also had the foresight to realize that as soon as the U.S. became involved in the war, all construction would be restricted to supporting the war effort. Accordingly, he acquired well over a thousand bathroom/kitchen fixture sets and sequestered them in storage. At war's end, when demand for housing was at its peak, Stu's father was one of the few builders in New York who had that rare commodity, fixtures—a fact he leveraged to the hilt.

Next generation (1964, thirty-five years later)

My employer, Lincoln Labs MIT in Massachusetts, had difficulty recruiting senior engineers to work at Kwajalein, the Missile Test Site in the mid-Pacific, 2,250 miles west of Honolulu. Potential candidates were skittish about working in such a remote locale due to the uncertainty of having a job upon their return.

I was young and confident that I could get a good job when I returned, so I jumped at the chance. Benefits included a 35% bonus, no income tax, and free housing. I also generated additional tax-free income by running a for-profit swim team 5 nights a week after work and teaching calculus two nights a week for the University of Hawaii extension.

After all expenses, I was able to save 110% of my base pay. This was my jumpstart, my nonlinear opportunity. Like my father and Stu's father a generation before, I saw an unusual opportunity and jumped on it, this time investing in rental houses.

More recently, Apple stock has had a spectacular run up in value, which has produced a large number of millionaires who gained their wealth with a small investment of a few thousand dollars and letting it run from there. The fundamentals were in place, and several acquaintances made the right choice. I have no idea how Bitcoin followed suit so there I missed the boat. I'm still waiting to see what will happen. You have to know yourself and what you're comfortable with. If I can't get my mind around an investment, I stay away. Being able to sleep at night has value too.

30.
THAT BEAUTIFUL BUICK

A year and a half into the war, my father decided it was time— time to begin feeding his stash of 300 top grade used automobiles through his showroom inventory. One thing he had not fully appreciated was that good tires on a car were often a bigger draw than the car itself.

One fall day in mid 1943, Mr. Jones, an impeccably well-dressed man, entered my father's showroom and strode past him as if he didn't exist, (*lowly order-taker not worth acknowledging*). He stopped in front of the most prestigious car in the place, if not in all of Minneapolis. My father had decided that very morning to bring his rare, high end, late-model, low-mileage Buick over from his warehouse inventory. The no-nonsense customer kicked one tire, turned to face my father, and proclaimed with great authority, "I'll take it. Get your manager!" *Done deal. Discussion not required.*

"Sure is a beaut, isn't she?" My father purposely drew out the discussion. *What's the hurry? You need me, far more than I need you.* "Came in hardly a few minutes ago. Knew it would generate a lot of interest the moment we put it out on the floor." *Not quite so fast mister alpha man. A little more "working the crowd" is called for here before we move on to the next stage.*

"I've been looking for a car like this for months—no success," volunteered Jones. "Nothing available in the whole damn city. Called my man in Milwaukee. Same as here—until now that is." *Okay, I'll play your little game, but keep it short. Need I remind you, I'm a very important man.* He then made a serious error by inadvertently displaying more interest in the car than he had intended by slowly sliding his fingers affectionately along the smooth finish of the hood. "And those tires. Look at them! Great tread. You just don't find tires like this nowadays. I'll take it. Where's your manager?" he continued in a more assertive, patronizing manner. His abruptness proclaimed, *Small talk is over. As I said, I'm a very busy man, so get on with it! Either you do it my way or get run over—your choice.*

"I am the manager."

"Should have known," Jones grimaced. "Cash or check?"

Now Jones was clearly a man of means, of prominence, a formidable adversary accustomed to getting his way. He was the total package: always in control, dominating each and every transaction, the perfect negotiator who could switch between white hat and black hat in a second. He instinctively knew when to flatter, when to threaten, and when to bully. But this time he failed to anticipate one tiny snag: the man standing between him and THE car, the man who held all the cards and knew it, my father.

My father had worked this overconfident customer into a less assured state of mind, which now allowed him to move the transaction to the next level.

"A check will do just fine. And oh, by the way," my father added, while feigning to scan the curb just outside his showroom, "I don't see your trade-in. Is it parked down the street? I need to look it over before we can close the deal."

Warning! Warning!

A cannonball has just been fired over your bow. You're about to be boarded by a man who in all appearances is a pushover—wrong! Best you raise the white flag. Cut your losses. Surrender immediately! I repeat. Surrender immediately!

"Trade-in?" blurted the now slightly less self-confident customer. This turn of events was totally unexpected. "What do you mean, 'trade-in'?"

"I have to have a trade-in to complete the transaction, Mr. Jones, or I'd be out of business," my father responded. "You understand. I have no problem selling everything the same day it comes through that door but, without trade-ins, my inventory would plummet to zero in less than a month—I'd be outta business."

"Forget the trade-in. I'll give you an extra four hundred bucks for the car. Here, take it!"

"Can't do that."

"Six hundred then!"

"Sorry, can't do that either," my father responded once again as he raised both palms and began to back away.

"What do you mean you can't do it? Of course you can. Here, just take the cash and give me the damn keys." Mr. Important Jones had just made a second crucial error. He betrayed that he had become overly attached to this one-of-a-kind prestigious Buick. He was now making decisions based strictly on emotions rather than logic. He had to have this car!

His position as top alpha dog was fading fast, which was not lost on either Jones or my father. And during their negotiations, two more impeccably dressed alpha types had entered the showroom and were drooling over The Buick—waiting for my father to be available. Jones knew there would soon be several more prospective buyers with loads of cash. He was in danger of losing his dream car.

My father now had total control over this transaction. He went on to explain, "The government has fixed the maximum prices, both for what I can sell and what I can pay for a car. If I violate these rules, even by a single dollar, I could be subject to huge fines and possibly even risk jail time. They send out undercover investigators to act as would-be customers all the time to entrap dealers. Can't chance it."

"But I have no trade-in. My ex-wife got the car in our settlement. What can I do?"

My father shrugged his shoulders and began to walk towards the next waiting customer leaving Jones dumbfounded. But—then my father slowed and turned: "You know what, though? I may have a possible solution. You say you have no trade-in, and I say I need you to have a trade-in to stay in business."

"Yeah, so?"

"So, what I can do is this. I'll sell you one."

"What do you mean, 'sell me one?'"

"See that '38 Ford over there? I can let you have it for $945."

"Then what?" replied the former alpha man, not bothering to hide either his disdain or his sarcasm. "I'm not sure just where this is leading, but it can't be good."

"Look, if you don't want to hear me out, that's ok. Probably wasn't a great idea anyway. Excuse me, I do need to take care of my other customers,"

As my father turned to take his leave once again, Mr. Jones quickly regained his composure.

"No, I apologize. That was rude of me. That's not like me. Please continue."

"Then you trade the Ford in on the Buick you have your heart set on. You will have the 'finest car available in all the Twin Cities,' and I'll have my trade-in."

Even though the alpha ranking had now been completely reversed, the customer couldn't help injecting another trace of sarcasm.

"And, if I may ask, just how much trade-in credit do you intend to give me for my wonderful newly acquired Ford?"

"Oh, I figure it should be worth at least $185 as a trade-in in today's market."

"That can't be legal!"

"Oh, that's where you're wrong. The government sets upper limits for how much I can buy or sell a car but sets no lower limits. I'll just write up the entire transaction as two separate sales. You buy the Ford for all cash at its legal upper limit and then buy the Buick at its legal upper limit with the Ford as trade-in with the rest in cash."

The well-heeled gentleman quickly glanced at the now three gentlemen waiting patiently in the wings and became red-faced as he realized he was about to be, not just skunked, but soundly skunked, by a lowly used car salesman. To my father's surprise, his expression suddenly flipped, and with a bellowing laugh and a slap on the back cried, "Ya know, you're good. You're very good. How would you like to come work for me? No one has ever worked me over that thoroughly before. You're a true master!"

They closed the deal on surprisingly cordial terms, and the new proud Buick owner quickly drove his prize out of the showroom down the street thinking, *Gotta get outta here before he insists I purchase a second trade-in as a trade-in on the first trade-in—and, oh my god, a third trade-in to buy the...*

He made one final mental note: *Never sit at the negotiating table across from that man. Either have him on your side or leave the room.*

31.
FOR SALE: 1940 FORD COUPE

–

LIKE NEW LOW MILEAGE GREAT TIRES BEST OFFER ABSOLUTELY NO OFFERS CONSIDERED BEFORE 8 AM

June 14, 1943

In rare opportunities like these, my father tried to time his arrival to be third out of the dozen prospective buyers (a few minutes before 8 am in this case) to pitch his offer to the private seller posting the ad. He'd chat with the seller for a minute or two to assess how best to meet his needs. Then he'd make his offer.

The seller confessed he was disappointed with what my father proposed. "That's the same amount those other two fellas offered me. I was hoping you could do a mite better."

"It's not us," my father explained. "It's the government. They control the top dollar we can pay. I personally think it's worth more, but none of us can risk going to jail or paying a big fine for offering more money."

"Well, thanks for coming," the seller responded. "Think I'll talk to a few more of these guys and take my chances. There seems to be a lot of interest in my car. Maybe one of them will sweeten his offer a bit."

My father knew he had just one shot to close this deal. It was now or never. During his size-up chat with the car owner, my father had put his Sherlock Holmes observation powers to work. To start with, he always studied the seller's fingers, to see if they were stained yellow—a telltale sign of a heavy smoker. Cigarettes were rationed and in short supply during the war, so to the chain smoker, they were often a stronger bargaining currency than money. My father always kept a couple dozen cartons of cigarettes in his trunk for situations just like this—another trick of the trade.

"Tell you what," my father interjected, "The wife's been all over me to quit smoking for months now. Just happened to have my last cigarette stash in my car—planned to give them to my brother-in-law who's always desperate. But, you know what? I'll throw them in. I believe it's just a bit over two cartons. Yeah, pretty sure that's right. I'll throw them in if you'd like—strictly as a goodwill gesture, mind you—not as part of the sale.

"I can tell you right now, I know all these guys and none of them dare offer a penny more for your car than what's on the table. And oh, even if you sell your car to one of these other buyers, be careful. See that short guy with the unbuttoned shirt holding his hat in his left hand—trying to look innocuous? I recognize him. He's a government consumer enforcement agent—one of their best. If someone makes an offer higher than what these other guys have already offered, and he's standing within earshot, just walk away and pretend you didn't hear it."

More often than not, my father was able to clinch a deal.

32.
WHERE'S YOUR FATHER, SONNY?

–

(THE WAR HAD ENDED SIX MONTHS EARLIER)

"Where's your father, Sonny?" This is not what a nine-year-old boy (me—and my name is not Sonny) wanted to hear from an imposing policeman (about nine feet tall, I reckoned). I was the sole occupant of the family car, illegally double-parked on a very busy street in downtown Minneapolis spring of 1946. Mr. Policeman accompanied his inquiry with a few intimidating raps of his baton across the palm of his hand, which only heightened my anxiety. My imagination projected my father and me arrested, handcuffed, and hauled straight off to jail.

Mr. Policeman kept a sharp eye on our car as he waited for my father to return. He strutted back and forth to give his best impersonation of a very important, no-nonsense official representative of the Minneapolis municipal government.

My father finally exited the adjacent store with a small package tucked under his arm and made straight for our car, ignoring Mr. Policeman altogether. I was too frightened to say anything and tried to shrink down to invisible. Mr. Policeman, however, would not be brushed off so easily. He approached from the driver side with a very solemn countenance and, to me at least, seemed even taller than before. Instead of pulling out his gun, calling for backup, and placing us both under arrest, he asked in as stern a voice as he could muster, "Mr. Jacobson, how am I doing on your new-car waitlist?"

Interpretation: "If you move me up on your waitlist, I'll overlook your blatant parking infringement this time."

My father looked Mr. Policeman straight in the eye and answered, "Now Mike, you know very well, it wouldn't be fair to let you jump ahead. You'll just have to wait your turn like everyone else."

Interpretation: "Mike, if you even think about giving me a parking ticket, your position on the list will plummet to the depths near never, which will add at least eight months to your wait. So don't mess with me— just go away!"

Flipping what I thought was a serious problem in less than thirty seconds made a huge impression on me. *Ah, so that's how they do it.*

Mr. Policeman backed off looking a bit sheepish. He was in over his head and wanted to withdraw from the playing field as quickly as he could. "Have a good day".

33.
CAR BUYERS HAVE LONG MEMORIES

–

THEN AGAIN, MAYBE NOT

"You'll destroy your future business if you treat customers that way. Customers don't forget and don't forgive." This was the gloomy prediction my father's rivals tried to saddle him with during heated sales technique debates towards the end of the war. They were referring to the techniques he developed in his automobile business—particularly his practice of requiring trade-ins with all high-end sales.

But within a few days of the war's end, as my father had foreseen, long lines popped up in front of every showroom in town. Potential buyers were anxious to get on the waitlists as soon as possible. Any sour memories of previous negotiations gone awry be damned. They wanted their car and they wanted it now, or at least as soon as possible. The resurrection of America's love affair with the automobile recovered full steam within minutes of armistice. Throughout the war there was full employment providing a steady stream of high wages and a surge of two-income families, but nothing to spend it on (except at dance studios, which didn't compete for war effort resources). Result: a large hoard of cash begging to be spent.

The three steps in many guys' minds were:
1) War's over.
2) Sailor, you may now kiss the girl in Times Square.
3) I want my car and I want it now!

When it was evident the war's end was in sight, the "Big Three" car manufacturers began to implement their return-to-peacetime business strategies. They needed to expand dealerships as quickly as possible to handle the expected explosive demand for cars and began to compete for potential dealers with proven track records. My father was quickly approached by Chrysler, as were several of his rival dealers. By the end of the first year following the war, the number of Dodge-Plymouth dealerships in the Twin Cities had grown to seven, including Jacobson Motors at 3038 Hennepin and Lake Street.

The next two years were undoubtedly the most profitable for those lucky enough to secure new car dealerships. Fewer sales positions were required than before the war, as job requirements were greatly simplified from highly skilled salesmen to barely literate order takers. To secure his place on a waitlist, a buyer would walk in, down payment check in hand, point to the car he wanted, and sign on the dotted line at list price with no attempt to haggle.

Due to a classic over-expansion in the industry, however, only two of the post war seven Dodge-Plymouth dealerships remained after my father threw in the towel in the late 1950s.

34.
MR. ANDERSON

Impeccably dressed, perfect posture, flawlessly groomed—Mr. Anderson was a man who could easily have been mistaken for a bank president as he strode confidently into a Minneapolis Cadillac showroom one Friday afternoon in the mid 1950s. It was as though, at least for him, a high-end car purchase was almost a non-event. For Mike, a salesman and former partner of my father's, Mr. Anderson was a gift from the gods, and he struggled not to salivate at what he hoped was about to transpire.

Mr. Anderson had his eyes glued on their featured automobile, an impressive, second-generation Cadillac Eldorado (produced from 1954 through 1956), by far the most expensive model in their inventory. He explained to Mike that he needed a luxury car in short order and, unless he could drive it off the lot that very afternoon, he would go to the dealer across town whom he understood had the same model in stock. He was willing to pay list price to move things along and would write out a check on the spot.

By the time the paperwork was completed and the check written, it was a few minutes past three, the time local banks then closed for the weekend.

Mike left the office and returned a few minutes later with the manager (the salesmen took turns playing "Manager" to maintain the white hat, black hat charade.)

"I do apologize, Mr. Anderson, but the bank has already closed, so we'll have to keep your vehicle over the weekend until we can verify your check has cleared. Company policy, you understand."

"But as I already explained to Mike here, it's mandatory that I have this vehicle this evening. I'm entertaining a very important client and… well never mind, I understand your position, but I'm afraid it doesn't meet my needs."

With that, Mr. Anderson retrieved the check from the manager's hand, ripped it in half, and added as he rose to leave, "I just have enough time for my driver to deliver me to Bergman's Cadillac over on the east side. Gentlemen, thank you for your time. Good day."

As Mr. Anderson reached the door, the manager caught up with him. Pretending not to notice the chauffeured stretch limo waiting outside, he called out, "Oh, Mr. Anderson? Please, I think we can work something out here, if you wouldn't mind stepping back into my office for a moment." Mr. Anderson glanced at his watch, gave the driver a nod as he raised his outstretched open palm with spread out fingers indicating five more minutes.

Mike and the manager quickly conferred in lowered voices while the buyer waited. "What's the risk? We'll make our full markup of 27% if the check clears and lose only repossession expenses if it doesn't. I say, let's go for it."

Thirty minutes later, Mr. Anderson released his driver and waved to the salesmen as he drove off behind the wheel of his new top of the line Cadillac.

The next morning, Mr. Anderson, now clad in worn jeans and a dirty shirt with holes in the sleeves, drove into a used car lot in a downscale neighborhood, across town from the dealership which had sold him the car.

"Can I help you, sir?" greeted the used car salesman.

"Yeah. I recently purchased this Cadi, but frankly, I'm not very happy with the ride. I've decided to dump it and get something that suits me better—but it has to be cash, since the banks aren't open—no checks."

The used car salesman low-balled Mr. Anderson and to his surprise, the offer was accepted with no hesitation— a bit too eagerly to the salesman's liking. He confided to his assistant, "I don't trust this guy—smells fishy to me. Better be careful until we get all the facts."

While Mr. Anderson removed a few personal effects from the car, the salesman had his assistant call the police department to verify it had not been reported stolen—standard procedure. No problem there, but when Jerry checked the papers that Mr. Anderson presented, he saw that the car had been procured only the day before. "Oops, thought so!" Both men agreed, red flags all over the place.

He called Mike, the salesman who had sold Mr. Anderson the car the previous day and discovered that Mr. Anderson's check had not yet cleared.

Fraud! Fraud! Fraud!

As Mike called the police, the salesman stalled Mr. Anderson on the pretext that they had to wait for an assistant to bring extra funds from their other location. The police arrived and arrested Mr. Anderson for fraud, writing a bad check, and attempting to sell stolen goods.

Later that day his lawyer argued before the judge that his client may be a bit idiosyncratic, but he had committed no crime. Nonetheless bail was denied. All players involved in Mr. Anderson's arrest congratulated themselves for being so vigilant. "Boy, that Mr. Anderson isn't very bright. Thought he could outfox us, did he? No way, ha!"

Monday morning, the bank opened on time and, surprise of surprises, the check cleared. Result: Mr. Anderson drove off from the courthouse in his brand new lien-free Cadillac. A false arrest suit was filed the following day. All parties settled for an undisclosed amount that covered the Cadillac, the lawyer's fees, Mr. Anderson's expenses, and a nice tidy *profit* that compensated him for his trouble, at least until he and his lawyer set up shop in his next target city.

35.
BORROWED EXPERTISE

My father, with years of experience, had developed an innate skill of optimally pricing his offers, which gave him a competitive edge over his competition. The downside of this skill was that several dealers would bounce customers off him to get a first estimate of true market value, then offer a few dollars more to steal the deal.

"I appreciate your giving us the opportunity to purchase your Lincoln, Mr. Louis, but at the moment we are overstocked on that particular model. However, you could try Mr. Jacobson at Jacobson Motors over on Lake and Hennepin. Last I heard, his Lincoln inventory was a bit low, and he's searching for models like yours.

"Tell you what though. Sometimes his offers can be a bit on the low side—particularly now that the war's been over for a while, the demand has finally been satisfied, and price controls are history. So, before you accept his offer, why don't you drop by and I'll tell you if you're leaving anything on the table."

Next day, Mr. Louis revisited the first dealer he had contacted with the news, "Mr. Jacobson came up with an offer of $470 for my car. Do you think that's a fair offer?"

"It's not too bad, but frankly a bit on the low side. Tell you what though. I can do a little better, say, $488. That's as much as you're likely to get anywhere in Minneapolis, and you'll save time driving around town trying to find a better deal."

"Sounds good, I'll take it."

36.
OBSERVING THE MASTER

I was about to take a major shift in my life's path and head off to college. The family consensus dictated I should be sent off properly with a newer, more reliable vehicle to make my long baggage-laden student treks between Minnesota and Massachusetts more comfortable and safer. My father, a retired auto dealer of a few years, offered to show me the ropes in finding a reasonably priced roadworthy used vehicle to replace my "piece of junk."

I was looking forward to our search because, while my father provided quite well for both myself and my brother, we seldom did anything together, and most of our conversations over the years lacked substance—mostly small talk. We were not close.

So off we went. As we walked onto our first used car lot, the salesman strolled over to greet us. He recognized my father immediately from the old days and stretched out his hand.

"Good to see you, Jake. Anything special I can help you with today?"

"No, Bruce, not just yet. Just going to look 'round a bit—kick a few tires."

"No problem, I'll be inside. Call me if I can be of any assistance."

Bruce guessed my father was looking for a car for me and let us begin our search. When my father located our first candidate, he raised the hood and checked the oil. "No good."

"Why not? Looks pretty clean to me. And we haven't even checked inside yet."

He wiped some oil from the dipstick between his thumb and first finger and explained, "The oil is S.A.E., 40 or more likely 50w (very heavy weight—high viscosity). You would only use oil this thick in a healthy motor for high speed desert driving where the high ambient temperature would overly thin a lighter weight oil (this was before multi-weight oils were introduced.) You'd never be able to start your car on a cold Minnesota winter morning with 50 weight oil—much too viscous. The starter would be overwhelmed and lock up even at ten degrees Fahrenheit. (I remember -41F in 1947.)

"In the case of this particular car, they changed to extra heavy oil to temporarily plug oil leaks and muffle serious engine noises. It tells me this car has a lot more wear than it appears. Poor compression—worn tappets. (Tappets convert the rotation motion of the camshaft to drive the valves.) Rings probably need to be replaced or worse, cylinders need to be re-bored. You don't want to touch this one."

We pushed on through the lot until we located a car that passed his oil weight criterion. He examined the front bumper. "Won't do."

Again, it looked ok to me, so I asked, "What do you see that you don't like?"

"There's a thin film of discoloration on the chrome in a pattern that only forms if it's been sitting on a lot for several weeks. Must have a bad ride or doesn't handle well—it's been rejected by all the test drivers so far. No reason to waste time on it."

Finally, we came upon a car that passed his first two criteria. He opened the door, looked at the pedals, and then studied the bottom of the doorstep where a driver would normally place his foot upon entering the car.

"Notice, the doorstep is worn significantly but the pedals have been changed to obscure its high mileage—standard trick of the trade. The heavily worn doorstep proves my point."

I checked the odometer—something I was surprised to observe my father had neglected to do. It read 23,000 miles, quite low for a vehicle reputed to be five years old. I was impressed.

Bruce, with time on his hands and curious as to what my father was up to, wandered out and joined us.

"Bruce, about 48,000 miles?"

"Closer to 51,000 miles if I remember right."

"*Now this makes no sense*," I thought and brought this ambiguity up with my father as we headed towards the next candidate lot. "The odometer said 23,000 miles; you said 48,000 miles and the sales guy confessed 51,000. How is that possible?"

"Well, the wear on the doorstep said 48,000 miles give or take a few thousand. Bruce told us 51,000 miles because he knew better than to lie to me, and the odometer reads 23,000 miles because it's been tampered with."

"You mean it's been set back?"

"Well, I suppose that's one way of looking at it. But most of the odometers on the newer cars are designed so they can't be set back to thwart that illegal practice. However, they can still be set forward. The usual procedure to reset an odometer is to connect a hand drill to the odometer drive cable slot and spin it fast forward. Instead of setting it back 20,000 miles for example, one sets it forward 80,000 miles." (In those days, odometers flipped over to zero at 100,000 miles.) "So technically no one sets an odometer back anymore, only forward. When you look at a used car on a sales lot, the least reliable information you'll encounter is the odometer reading—never bother to look at it."

I was clearly in the presence of a master.

"Also, a couple of those cars we skipped were owned by heavy smokers, which as a non-smoker, would get to you eventually and make it quite unpleasant for your passengers who don't smoke—girlfriends for example."

"I saw some of those ash tray stains too. But the smell didn't seem that bad."

"Another trick of the trade."

"Used car trick?"

"Yup. Every dealer has a spray can of 'new car smell' on hand, which they apply liberally so the stale air odor won't turn off prospective customers. Not unlike a realtor baking cookies during an open house. The presale odor usually resurfaces within a few weeks—or ten minutes after the new buyer drives his dream car off the lot."

We ended up buying a new car—there was less to worry about. I didn't feel we wasted time looking at used cars though as I did get a great "Used Car Purchase 101" education and learned a little more about what made my father tick.

When my parents retired in 1957, they purchased a modest, ground floor, beachfront condo near Fort Lauderdale, Florida. They occupied the unit from early January to mid-April (New Years to income tax time.) They would drive first to the Mayo Clinic in Rochester for complete physicals, don their snowbird hats, and continue on to Florida. My mother was scared of planes because of a terrifying biplane joyride on a blind date in her early twenties and wasn't coaxed into flying a second time for forty years. Once flying became a viable option, they needed to secure wheels for the four months they remained in Florida.

"What to do?" Not a problem. Every year my father would rent a car while he scouted around to buy a three to five year-old Caddy, then four months later, reverse the process and sell the car at a profit the day they returned home to Minnesota. The layman buyer however, would shell out a couple thousand dollars above market during the buy transaction and sell the vehicle for a couple thousand dollars below market value during the sell transaction.

37.
OOPS, SOMETHING AWRY

–

EARLY 1950s

It was all routine enough. A well-dressed, distinguished, middle-aged man drove his late model Dodge onto my father's lot to inquire if my father were interested in purchasing his vehicle.

"I've been promoted. But on condition that I transfer to Cleveland. The good news is that my company will provide me with new wheels once I get there."

"Sounds like a great opportunity," (my father always used small talk to get a better understanding of prospective customers.)

"Yeah, it really is. After fifteen years, I finally made management. I was scheduled to move out at the end of next month, but the guy I'm replacing had a heart attack, so they need me there pronto. They're giving me a nice sized bonus if I can get there by Monday, and since I'll no longer need my current car, I decided to sell it rather than drive it out."

A test drive didn't uncover anything wrong with the car beyond normal wear and tear, so it looked like a no-brainer to my father.

"Looks like you took real good care of your car."

"Always do. Love my cars. I think it's a real crime when someone doesn't maintain their vehicle properly."

"Well, it looks like we can do business here. Be right back."

He excused himself for a minute and called the police from an adjacent office to ensure it had not been reported stolen—standard practice as Minnesota did not issue proof of title in those days. Satisfied, my father checked at the car over one last time and returned to the seller. "Real clean. But your trunk is locked, and I don't see the key here on the key chain."

"Those are my spares. Lost the trunk key about a week ago at the beach. I can run over to a locksmith and get one made if you like."

My father thought, *"Once this guy leaves the lot, I'll never see him again. It's either accept the risk or say goodbye to the deal."*

My father had had a long and successful track record of assessing his customers upfront, so he took the chance and made an executive decision: *"I'll stall him another 15 minutes before I hand him a check, then verify with the police one last time. Besides, for a check this size, the bank is supposed to call me first before they honor it. That gives me an additional half hour."*

A price was agreed upon, a second call to the police showed no problem, and the payment exchanged hands to complete the sale.

As soon as the customer left, my father summoned his usual locksmith and within twenty minutes the trunk was opened exposing its content.

"Not good," my father told his locksmith as they peered into the trunk.

"Why, Mr. Jacobson? What's wrong?"

"Look, there's a new outboard motor in here—it's way too valuable to forget."

One more call confirmed his fears. The car had just been reported stolen a minute earlier. A quick call to the bank yielded more bad news—the customer (or rather, now the thief) had just left the bank with his cash in hand.

"George," my father lectured the assistant bank manager, "you know our deal. You're to call me before you cash a check that large."

"Well, Mr. Jacobson, I'm truly sorry. We're shorthanded today and had to use some tellers in training. Then too, today is payday for most people around here so things have been more hectic than usual."

When my father told me this story, I asked, "So, what did you do—eat the loss?"

"Oh no, I sued the bank. It's not legal to cash a check issued on a stolen vehicle."

"But they had no way of knowing the car had been stolen! Weren't you supposed to verify that, not them? And besides, you're the one who issued the check. You said you only had a verbal agreement with the bank that they call you when a large check is presented for payment. But from what I understand, the agreement was not even written down."

"Actually, we settled after a single letter from my attorney. The bank understood that due to precedent, they were partly at fault. And they knew it was to their advantage to do whatever it took to keep me happy and keep my business. For years I've been referring all the financing generated by my sales to them. I did receive referral finder's fees, but the bank fully comprehended it'd be easier for me to move my business to another bank than for them to replace the lost business if I were to do so."

"So, what was the final outcome?"

"We split the loss fifty-fifty and continued as if nothing happened."

38.
CREATIVE SOLUTIONS

The first two hundred feet of road access from the main road to our home on Lake Minnetonka was legally a public road. The continuation then split into three separate private driveways. Our portion made a sharp turn to the right, wound down a very steep hill, and finally circled past our front door before it retraced its return route back up the hill.

Whenever more than a few inches of snow accumulated on our sharp, curved, steep driveway (up to twenty inches during particularly harsh Minnesota winters), it became a challenge to navigate the route back up to the main road without landing in a ditch. On a bad snow day, if one approached the hill too slowly the tires would lose their grip and start to spin halfway up bringing the car to a complete halt just short of the top. If one attacked the hill too aggressively, the centrifugal force at the bend would push the car sidewise into the ditch midway through the curve. To figure out the perfect speed required to conquer the hill took me several weeks of trial and error and steady nerves.

Almost monthly we would be snowed in for days at a time. Unfortunately for me, even with the heaviest snows, our school was very stingy with "snow days," so I was still expected to trudge up the hill to catch my bus.

Our local county snowplow driver was obligated to clear the snow off the first two hundred feet of the public access portion that led to our shared driveways. He would then, with great difficulty, back out onto the main road to continue his road clearing. The clearing of the private driveways fell to the individual families, which meant either tough manual shoveling by my brother and me or by costly hired snow removal labor. This obstacle, however, was a piece of cake for my father.

Beginning the third winter after we moved into our lakeside home, I noticed that the snowplow no longer stopped and backed out after reaching the 200-foot public/private driveway transition. Instead, it continued down our private, treacherous driveway, clearing snow as it went. Then it paused halfway around the circle near our front door, at which time my father would stroll out and chat with the driver for about thirty seconds. *Oh*, I thought, *that's nice, my father is so friendly with the snowplow driver—probably complimenting them on the great job they're doing.*

When neighbors questioned my father about why the plow driver altered his route and coincidently cleared the snow from our driveway as he circled around the loop, my father would respond, "Oh, I gave him permission to use our circle to turn around so he wouldn't have to back up the 200 feet to the county road—it's easier and much safer. The driver is quite grateful for this arrangement."

The truth came out when I was 14. My father decided I should take over the "friendly driver chat responsibilities" for the family. That was when I discovered the "little chat" included something in an unmarked brown bag to warm the driver during his difficult rounds—such a kind gesture. Problem solved, provided of course, the driver didn't get blurry-eyed and run off the road from consuming too much "kind gesture."

39.
BOUNDARIES

–

IT'S A GUY THING

"One more gate and we're there!"

Even after returning each summer for forty-five years, I still got butterflies when we drove through this last gate onto our land, or *The Land* as we called it.

My wife, Meimei, and I were visiting our private piece of Colorado paradise (9,000 ft elevation, forty miles due west of Colorado Springs) for the first time that year. It occupies 190 acres on the north slope of Thirty Nine Mile Mountain overlooking Eleven Mile Reservoir. We are always excited just to be there. We purchased this property fifteen months after we first met while I was a grad student at the University of Colorado in Boulder and Meimei an administrator in the same building. Buying this property was the culmination of a year of weekend searches. With our final payment fifteen years later, we owned it free and clear—all ours! We pulled a small trailer with a tiny kitchen and double bed onto the land to make it more comfortable. This offered us a monthly respite from city pressures and any negative energy piled up throughout the week. It was so quiet and the terrain so spacious, you could hear a fly buzz 100 yards and one hill over.

That was three years before our unanticipated move to northern California so Meimei could attend Stanford Business School. Our move was intended to be a brief two year detour for us, maybe 20 months at the most—not the 45 year hiatus we've enjoyed thus far.

"I suppose you're off to do the usual," was Meimei's first comment after she closed the last gate behind us.

"Well, of course," I confirmed—"have to!"

"I really don't understand," she interjected, "why you feel compelled to walk the entire boundary the moment we arrive. Couldn't it wait until tomorrow?"

"No. Gotta be done right away. It's in the Colorado boundary walking manual. It's a guy thing—can't be explained. Either you understand it, or you don't."

"Does that mean you're going to mark all the boundaries as well?"

"Well of course, that too, well at least the corners—have to stay in good standing with the National Boundary Marking Society, NBMS, (a wolf is their mascot.) I do admit though that as I get older, producing enough marking fluid to cover the critical boundary points gets tougher every year. Last year I forgot to drink enough water on our way here and lost several points in my standing."

Protecting Property Lines

Our home on Lake Minnetonka, St Albans Bay where I lived from third grade until college, had 500 feet of wonderful clear shoreline. We moved there in the fall of 1946 at the end of WWII. I was nine at the time and immediately took on the self-assigned goal of knowing every pond, shoreline feature, turtle, back road, and tree within a mile of our house either by canoe, foot, or my Doodle Bug motor scooter powered by a Briggs and Stratton lawn mower motor (top wind-aided, slightly downhill speed on a good day was 28 mph.) Fifteen years later, as empty nesters living on savings, my parents decided to improve their liquidity and sold off two surveyed buildable lots, one on either side of their house—each with 150 feet of lake frontage, retaining 200 feet for themselves. Both new lots sported a fancy lakefront home within a year.

Unfortunately, our bachelor neighbor to the south, Mr. Williamson, was an extreme alpha male. As the manager of a very large, high-end, and successful motel complex in Minneapolis, the Thunderbird Motel, he exploited his position of power to extensively landscape his new house at the corporation's expense—it was just a matter of how he handled the invoices.

In the process, he took the liberty of extending his landscaping onto our property by a good twenty five feet. He rationalized that *since his landscaping improved our property as well, and we never seemed to use that portion anyway, he did nothing amiss—in fact he did us a favor.*

He carried this imposition even further by consistently leaving much of his ground grooming equipment, such as rakes, wheel barrels and trash, up to fifty feet further into our side of the shared boundary. Mr. Williamson's pushiness and lack of courtesy greatly perturbed my father.

My father did not see it Mr. Williamson's way. It was obvious that Mr. Williamson's aggressive move onto our property was to make his house more grandiose at our expense and possibly establish a case for eventual eminent domain.

Two alpha males in disagreement usually does not bode well. After several letters addressing their differences, Mr. Williamson was unwilling to compromise even the slightest amount—not because of the expense involved but to prove he was more alpha than my father. He clearly thrived on confrontation and was used to getting his way.

My father was of the ilk who incorporates the "Four-step Negotiation Rule." It's quite simple really:

1) Compromise
2) Compromise
3) Compromise
4) Kill!

"I'll pay you an extra hundred bucks if you show up to install the 6-foot chain link fence no earlier than 7:45 am and be outta here leaving no trace by 6:30 pm." (Mr. Williamson always left for work at 7:30 am and returned home no sooner than 6:45 pm.) My father wanted to give Mr. Williamson no advance notice of his intentions.

"Yes, Mr. Jacobson," replied the contractor. I'll put a couple extra men on it."

The contractor was enthusiastic about the job as his bid was a full 50% above market to begin with. As promised, by 6:30 pm, a shiny, new chain link fence separated the entire length of the two properties with no trace of workmen or equipment remaining.

As expected, Mr. Williamson showed up pounding furiously on our door at 6:50 pm that evening, red-faced, fuming with his rapid high pitched tirade peppered voice, which included a high percentage of low information content expletives.

"You know what your god-damned fence people did to my garden? How dare you build a fence without consulting me! Just who do you think you are? I'm going to sue your ass off for trespassing! You…"

This barrage of threats continued as the two adversaries crossed our yard to the fence (jostling each other's shoulders as they went.) "Look here," Mr. Williamson ranted, "your goddamn fence cuts right through my garden!"

Finally, my father responded, "I am totally within my rights as this fence is six inches on my side of the surveyed property line. And correction, the fence does not cut through your garden, it separates your garden from what is now my garden, and items you had strewn on my property have been relocated onto your property where they belong. Furthermore, I shall consider anything you leave on my side in the future to be abandoned, and shall as such, dispose of as I see fit. Now, you are trespassing on my property, so please leave."

Even more red-faced, Mr. Williamson stomped off.

Nothing was heard from him for the next few weeks but then, in defiance and perhaps to salvage some face, Mr. Williamson began to store his garden hoses strung out along the top of the joint fence like a long snake with half hanging on our side and half on his side.

My father did nothing for two weeks to convince himself this was not a one time oversight but a purposeful act of defiance. One day after Mr. Williamson left for work, my father decided it was time—time to act. He calmly took a saw from our tool shed and cut off those portions of the hoses that hung on our side of the fence, leaving the remaining severed half-loops clinging to Mr. Williamson's side of the fence. We never heard from our neighbor to the South again.

Males have defended their boundaries for at least the last 100,000 years. It's a guy thing.

40.
A PENNY FOR YOUR THOUGHTS

In the summer of 1904, my father, who was nine at the time, coveted several penny treats that called to him from the local candy store's display window. He asked his mother if he could do some chores around the house to earn some money to buy candy. She offered him several options, most of which didn't appeal to him. He finally settled on scrubbing the white boardwalk that led from the gate to their front door—at least it was outside. Several times when he was sure he had satisfactorily completed his assigned task, his mother's critical eye spotted defects in his work, which he had to make right if he expected to get paid.

Finally, after several hours, she approved his work, opened her purse, and pulled out a single penny—not exactly what he had hoped for. Nonetheless, he took possession of the penny and headed off to the candy store to quench the desire that had held his thoughts while scrubbing away under the hot sun.

There were at least a dozen candidates that vied for his attention, either for a penny each or two for a penny. He weighed his prospects carefully. After long and intense consideration of his options, he stood up, slipped the penny back into this pocket, and left. Suddenly that penny, for which he had spent the whole afternoon working, was far more valuable to him than the candy which would last at best ten seconds.

41.
AUNT BEA

Aunts and uncles tend not to be particularly interesting to a twelve-year old, especially if they visit less than once a year. After all, they are a full generation apart and have very little in common except for shared relatives. It's both their faults; it's neither of their faults.

It's the twelve-year old's fault because she/he doesn't ask the aunt/uncle any questions; it's the aunt/uncle's fault for not encouraging the twelve-year old to ask any questions. It's not the twelve-year old's fault, because they lack the experience to communicate with adults; it's not the aunt/uncle's fault because they're convinced a twelve-year old can't answer anything beyond "Do you like school?" "What do you want to be when you grow up?" or "What is your favorite subject in school?

It's the Auntie Mame and Mary Poppins-type aunts who can make all the difference. My father's younger sister, Aunt Bea, was one such aunt. Even though I'd been in her company only three times in my life (once in Minnesota and twice in California), she made a major impression on me. She was out there! She knew how to live!

They grew up as lower middle class kids in Swea City, a small town in Iowa. My father wanted to have things whereas Aunt Bea wanted to have experiences. He dropped out of school at fourteen, partied in his twenties, bought luxury items in his forties, and worked 14 hours a day in his fifties to gain prosperity and status. She, on the other hand, graduated nursing school, spent all her spare money on dance lessons, traveled whenever she could, and didn't give a hoot what people thought about how she lived her life.

When WWII broke out, she and her doctor husband, Uncle Ruben Swenson, volunteered to manage a small medical base in Fiji in the South Pacific where they served for most of the war. They shared incredible experiences, but since I never asked the right questions, I never learned the details. I do remember that she talked about being the only outsider attending Fijian boar tusk ceremonies. If only I had asked!

After WWII, they settled in San Francisco near Chinatown on Taylor St., Nob Hill. Following a Boy Scout Jamboree on the Irvine Ranch in Southern California in 1953 (I was just sixteen,) I spent two weeks with her in San Francisco (Uncle Ruben was away). I became an expert San Francisco Street explorer, which included covering the length of Chinatown every day.

"Lynn, I'm out of paper napkins for dinner. Here, take this money and run down to the store down at the corner and get me some." *Well, I want to be helpful and readily accepted. After all, how hard can it be to buy a bunch of stupid paper napkins?* I took the bills she held out to me and set off for the corner mom and pop store.

The task turned out to be a bit trickier than I anticipated. Examining the displays, I discovered there were two types of napkins, ordinary paper napkins and sanitary napkins. *This shouldn't be too difficult. I'm sure Aunt Bea wants me to get only the best napkins available, and because the sanitary napkins are the more expensive of the two, they're the obvious choice.* I further reasoned, *Why would anyone buy unsanitary napkins, anyway?*

Yes, I had to return to the store and exchange my purchase—how embarrassing for a sixteen-year old male to expose his stupidity under the gaze of a smug young clerk.

During the last week of my stay in San Francisco, Dick, my three-year older brother, flew out to join us. My father, being an auto dealer, arranged for one of his used cars to be sent out from Minnesota in which the three of us drove back to Minnesota (Aunt Bea stayed with us for a couple of weeks, then flew back to San Francisco.) One of the reasons for driving rather than flying back to Minnesota was for me to practice driving. A second was for us to see some of the most spectacular western mountain country. Driving through Wyoming was a piece of cake, long, straight and not too crowded. This was my big chance. I happily took the wheel with my Aunt Bea riding shotgun while my brother overstuffed the back seat with his 6' 3" frame. To get more comfortable during a nap in this small car, he removed his shoes and stuck his feet out the rear window. For the next 100 miles everyone settled in, and I became perhaps a bit too complacent congratulating myself on a "job well done."

It seemed my passing skills were not as polished as I thought. On one particularly clear stretch of road, I swung out to pass a large truck. Two thirds through the pass, my brother suddenly jumped up, shoved his dirty socked foot in my face and shouted, "Look what you've done, you dumb ass!" (My brother had a limited vocabulary.) He showed me his sock-covered foot, which was now quite grimy.

"Get that thing out of my face—I can't see—and it's not my fault you didn't put on clean socks this morning!" At the same time I glanced back at the truck I had just passed; there was a new clean streak along its side. Oops.

That was the last time my brother ever took a nap with his feet sticking out of the rear seat window—at least when I was at the wheel.

In many medical families, the heavily time-pressured doctor did the doctoring and the spouse/partner took care of their family finances. Following the war, as life settled down to a steady and prosperous pace, Aunt Bea and Uncle Ruben followed suit. Aunt Bea decided she wanted to open a dress shop. After several months of searching for an ideal location, she took what looked like a good opportunity and made it into a great opportunity—the dress shop at the St. Francis Hotel on Union Square. It was available, furnishings and all for $15,000 including two antique tables in the inventory. She then:

1) Bought the dress shop for $15,000 including the antique tables.
2) Sold the two tables to a wealthy friend for $15,000.
3) The friend had the tables appraised for $25,000.
4) Friend donated the tables to a museum and took a write off.
5) Friend grossed $22,750 tax savings (top tax bracket was over 90% in the 1950s.)

Result: Sellers got their asking $15,000. Aunt Bea owned the dress shop at no net cost to herself. Friend was ahead by $7,750. Museum was ahead by two beautiful antique tables.

THE PHENOMENAL MR. H. M. LUI,
UNCLE-IN-LAW

Mr. H. M. Lui, Uncle-in-law

1972
Luis and Pans at
Luis's Daughter's Wedding

42.
YOUR PARENTS WOULD NEVER FORGIVE ME...

"You don't have to take me to the airport, Uncle. Please, I can get there just fine by myself—really. I've done it many times before."

"Oh, but I MUST," insisted Mr. Lui (Uncle Lui to Meimei). "Your parents would never forgive me if anything should happen to you. You see, I have no choice," he continued with arms stretched out, palms facing upward as if this gesture alone should clinch the discussion.

It was 1968 and Meimei (a college sophomore) had just finished her winter break visiting her parents in Hong Kong. She was working out her transportation options to get to Kai Tak International airport for her return flight home. Her father was quite ill, and her mother attended to him full time, so Mr. Lui, a long-time close family friend, decided to take charge of getting Meimei to the airport—to ensure she reached the airport without incident.

The Pan and Lui families had been close for many years, ever since Mr. Pan had "fired" Mr. Lui some thirty-five years earlier (1930s in mainland China).

"No arguing, Meimei. I pick you up promptly tomorrow morning—eight o'clock. Please be ready."

"Okay, Uncle, but you needn't wait with me. I've done this before. I know how to handle all the check-in details and stuff. Just drop me off."

Mr. Lui's head nodded affirmative, but the mischievous twinkle in his eyes bespoke otherwise.

Mr. Lui was not Meimei's blood uncle, but rather an uncle in the Asian sense of the word, used to show respect with uncle-like bonding. When a male is addressed as Uncle (or female as Auntie), even if the age gap is small, both parties understand that a familial bond with unwritten obligations exist between the two.

The next morning, Meimei paced agitatedly until Mr. Lui finally arrived, nearly half an hour late, and they did not actually leave her parents' home for another fifteen minutes (to show them respect.) That gave her barely an hour to reach the airport, check in, and board her scheduled international Pan Am flight.

"I'll miss my flight! It's too late!"

"No need to worry. You have my word. You will make your flight."

"But…"

"It does no good to worry over what you cannot change. My driver—very skilled—knows all the shortcuts and tricks. Nobody can get us there faster."

She fell silent but did not in the least buy into this reassurance. Instead, she stared morosely at the prominent HM (Mr. Lui's initials) hood ornament on his top-of-the-line black Mercedes and awaited her fate.

Upon reaching Kai Tak airport in East Kowloon (resituated to Lantau Island in 1998), the car merged adroitly through the quagmire of aggressive vehicles, all vying for the limited access to disgorge anxious passengers at the departure doors. Meimei reached for her suitcase to make a dash for it when Mr. Lui held her back. "No. Not so fast. Mr. Lee here will see to it that your bag is checked in properly and your ticket secured—all arranged." It was then that she first noticed the tall, well-dressed older man with perfect posture who was strolling off with her tiny, ancient, and very worn bag.

Before she had time to think, the driver advanced the vehicle a few hundred yards further down the curb to where the parking competition thinned and doors could be opened safely. Mr. Lui exited the vehicle with Meimei in tow, "Come! Come this way." He escorted her down a long hall into the airport's Miramar restaurant with no explanation—then even further through a second unmarked door into a small private dining area. This more elegant inner dining room had three small tables—the largest of which was set for two. Mr. Lui ignored Meimei's protests. "This is the wrong way! I saw my gate. It's that way, to the right. I'm sure I'll miss my plane!"

He bade her sit and ordered some breakfast from the waiter who was so attentive that it was obvious he had been awaiting their arrival. A great amount of food arrived within minutes.

"I don't have time to eat!" Meimei objected. "I'm not hungry," she lied. "My plane is leaving. I must get back to school. Please!" she begged—almost to tears.

"You have time. Must eat. If you board on an empty stomach, you become ill. Your parents would never forgive me if I let that happen. I'd lose face. Please, you must eat."

A cyclical one-act play then ensued where Meimei would protest, Mr. Lui would insist, Meimei would take a token bite followed by another protest, Mr. Lui would insist, Meimei would… This routine was repeated until a frantic Meimei finally convinced her abductor she was quite sated and was no longer in danger of passing out from severe food deprivation on her flight home.

They left the restaurant and turned towards her departure gate. To Meimei, it seemed ten miles away. She began to run, an involuntary reaction once she spotted the clock on the wall that warned it was now 20 minutes past her scheduled departure time.

"No, no, Meimei. No! Must not run. Upset stomach! If you get sick on the flight running so soon after eating, your parents would never forgive me…"

How many times is he going to play that card? she wondered after she slowed to a fast walk or at least as fast as she could manage under Mr. Lui's close supervision.

She finally approached her gate at the end of the corridor, and to her surprise, saw a couple hundred passengers milling about. No one had yet boarded!

Oh thank God. Must be a weather delay, she thought, almost giddy with relief. But then the tall, well-dressed man who had taken her bag earlier reappeared. It was at this moment she realized all was not as it seemed.

"Mr. Lee, see to it that Miss Pan gets safely to her seat and is comfortable."

"Certainly, sir."

And with that, Mr. Lee offered her his arm and duly escorted her past all the ticket agents, VIPs, first-class, and gawking economy passengers. There were perhaps as many as 400 eyes tracking this young passenger trying to decipher "Who is this girl?" as she was escorted onto the plane and midway down the aisle to her low budget economy seat. If her ticket had been any less expensive, she probably would have had to serve drinks.

Mr. Lee projected such authority that even the Pope or the President would have deferred to him. "Can I get you anything? A pillow or perhaps something to drink?" Mr. Lee inquired solicitously with no signs of being rushed.

"No, no. I'm fine. Really! Everything is perfect. Thank you so much. Couldn't be better."

"Perhaps a magazine?"

"No, no, I have one. Thanks all the same."

At this point, Mr. Lee, unable to suppress his smile any longer, turned away so as not to embarrass her. He approached the plane's exit and signaled the attendants that the VIPs and first-class passengers could now board.

Over the hubbub amongst the passengers as they filed in could be heard, "Who is that young woman?" "Must be a movie star." "Someone said he thought she was a prince's daughter—or maybe an ambassador's daughter." "Whoever she is, she's gotta be really important." "Yeah, must be. I saw two movie stars waiting for her to board."

The other passengers were then allowed to board. As they filed past this young sprig with her head buried deep behind her magazine, they looked puzzled but were clearly impressed. No one talked to her that entire flight, but they did sneak glances in her direction when they thought she wouldn't notice. She garnered more attention from the flight attendants on that flight than all the first-class passengers combined.

"Who is that girl?"

When her father heard her story, he couldn't stop laughing.

"Meimei, didn't HM tell you where all his pull came from?"

"No. He never even hinted that he had actually held my flight just so I could have breakfast—that's what he did, wasn't it?"

"Yes, that's his way. He should have at least let you know that he is on the Board of Directors of Pan Am and owned the restaurant you breakfasted at. That's why he didn't hesitate to promise you would make your flight. He could have held it all week if he wanted to."

43.
THE PAN/LUI CONNECTION
—
(EARLY 1930s)

"You wished to see me, Mr. Pan?"

"Yes, Mr. Lui. Please won't you come in? Have a seat."

Mr. Lui had anticipated this meeting with great anxiety for several weeks. He was pretty sure how it would end, and from his perspective it was *not* good.

Mr. Pan began, "Mr. Lui, I'm sure you remember our last conversation a few months ago when I told you your talents, although many and admirable, are wasted here. They are more suited for business than banking."

"Yes, sir. But I've done so much better since then."

"No. You've worked harder and kept longer hours, but not better. I strongly feel you should pursue an alternate career—one that can fully utilize your talents. Trying to emulate your father-in-law's successful banking career has little chance of success. You're a round peg trying to fit into a square hole."

"But Mr. Pan, I am about to start a family, and I need this job!"

"I've given your situation considerable thought. Let's face it, you are an entrepreneur, not a banker."

"But sir!"

"Wait! Please hear me out. Take some time and think it through. See what may be out there for you. You mentioned you were considering purchasing a candy factory with your friend, Mr. Chiu. Is that still an option?"

"Yes sir, but I have very little savings and couldn't go without income for as long as it would take to get it off the ground."

"The bank will carry you for a few months to give you time to further explore your options without distraction. Would that be sufficient to evaluate your candy factory options?"

Mr. Lui was taken aback by such generosity, rare for its time. "Thank you so much, Mr. Pan. I appreciate what you are doing to help me. Yes, that should do it."

Mr. Lui was hesitant to leave his bank job because he had grown up in extreme poverty. He feared jeopardizing what little security he had thus far established for himself and his soon-to-be family. His childhood beginnings were so poor that at one time, he and his two youngest siblings had to share a single pair of outside shoes among them—girl's shoes at that. As Mr. Lui later lectured his children, "When the choice is between girl's shoes and no shoes, the decision is a no brainer."

A few weeks after their meeting, Mr. Lui updated Mr. Pan concerning his candy factory opportunity. Thus, with Mr. Pan's further encouragement, Mr. Lui began his new life as a true entrepreneur.

Mr. Lui and his wife worked sixteen-hours a day, seven days a week at their factory where they slept on cots in the back room to save time and money. Their sacrifice allowed them to reinvest the small initial profits into increased inventory, equipment, and expanded manufacturing floor space.

Mr. Pan proved to be prophetic—after a few years, the Luis prospered far beyond even his expectations. Mr. Lui leveraged the candy business and expanded into textiles, Hong Kong real estate including the hotel industry and investing in U.S. equity. Forty-five years after that fateful day when Mr. Pan, in so many words "fired" him, Mr. Lui was acknowledged to be one of the most astute and successful businessmen in Hong Kong.

Upon his death, he committed the majority of his vast wealth to establish the largest charitable family foundation in Hong Kong with a particular focus on medicine.

The Pan and Lui families stayed in touch over the years following the end of WWII via Christmas cards, even though the Pans moved to Cincinnati, Ohio and the Luis stayed in Hong Kong. After the Pans returned to Hong Kong in 1968, Mrs. Pan and Mrs. Lui, (one month apart in age), confided in one another that they hoped the Luis' middle daughter, Felicia, then attending college in London, and the Pans' son, Enlin, Jr., attending graduate school in New York City, might meet.

Their opportunity came a few years later when the Luis' daughter, accompanied by her oldest brother, planned a trip to New York to explore graduate school options in the U.S. (similar to Emma's search thirty-one years earlier on the California coast.)

Felicia later explained to the author: "I wanted to explore graduate school opportunities in the U.S. Every young person in those days wanted to travel to New York. Not wanting my father involved in my trip plans, I contacted my older brother, Alex, who was in summer school in South Carolina and suggested he accompany me to explore New York and Washington, D.C. Since I wanted to be independent, and because of my limited funds from my summer jobs, I planned a low travel budget which included camping and budget hotels."

"Look, Alex, here on the map! There's a big green section in the center of New York! It must be woods or something" (Central Park.) "We can save a lot of money by camping there— we can build a fire to cook and save even more."

This did not seem so out of the norm to these two young travelers, as camping in parks was common practice in Europe during the early seventies. New York City at that time, however, was another matter.

When Mr. Lui told the Pans of his children's New York plans, the Pans were horrified. "Yikes! Say goodbye to them both! You'll never see them again." They conjured up all sorts of extreme dangers: robbery, kidnapping, murder, or worse. Upon reflection, however, both couples realized that their kids' camping plans, in truth, presented an opportunity.

A frantic long-distance call that night from Mr. Lui to Alex and Felicia followed by a similar call from Mr. Pan to his son, Enlin, kept Felicia and Alex from being 'tragic murder victims' headlines.

Fortuitously, the Pans' son was living in their New York Lincoln Towers apartment on West End Avenue and had a spare room for the would-be campers. Arrangements were worked out. The final coup de gras that convinced Felicia and Alex to accept the Pans' offer was: "Don't worry about disturbing Didi (Enlin Jr). He is quite reclusive and spends all day on his thesis. You'd be lucky to get ten words a day out of him during the entire length of your stay."

This last sentence was in serious error. One glance at Felicia and poof, no more reclusiveness!

Result: Marriage four years later.

44.

AUNTIE LUI

Even though Mrs. Lui's father had been a successful banker in Shanghai and Hong Kong, she herself never liked banks.

"Ma'am! Oh Ma'am! You left this bag at my counter." The salesclerk at the Stanford Shopping Mall had to run nearly a city block to overtake my wife, Meimei, and Mrs. Lui.

"Ma'am! You left this paper bag on my counter. I was afraid it might be important and wanted to get it back to you before the janitor dumped it in the trash."

Mrs. Lui thanked the winded clerk with a smile and slight bow. She handed the bag to Meimei and said, "Here, you carry it for a while. I keep leaving it behind." The Luis were visiting Palo Alto so that Mr. Lui could undergo medical procedures at the Stanford Hospital. While they waited for treatments to be completed, Meimei accompanied Mrs. Lui to the nearby shopping center for some recreational shopping. Meimei thought nothing of Mrs. Lui's misplaced paper bag until she happened to glance inside—it was stuffed full of $100 bills, perhaps $20,000 worth. Thereafter, Meimei clutched the bag firmly in both arms while she accompanied Mrs. Lui the rest of the day. She constantly scanned her surroundings for suspicious looking muggers, ignoring the plethora of enticing products screaming from every counter for her attention.

Several years later Mrs. Lui's daughters confirmed that such mishaps had taken place before. A friend of Mrs. Lui had been shopping in a Hong Kong department store when she spotted Mrs. Lui asleep in a waiting room with a shopping bag fallen over at her feet. Next to the bag were several rolls of large bills splayed on the floor around her. She woke Mrs. Lui and helped her round up the money.

Whenever Mrs. Lui would visit Mrs. Pan in Palo Alto, the extended family would share a dinner at an authentic Chinese restaurant—all sitting around a large round table. After a few visits, we could predict two parts of the evening. The first was there would be enough food ordered to satisfy three times as many diners as were actually present. Even after valiant efforts of the extended family, the leftovers would provide us enough calories for a full week.

The second event was the entertainment provided by Mrs. Lui and Mrs. Pan in their attempts to outdo each other, one arm blocking the other lady, stacking food on the other's plate. They spent more time jostling than eating. By dinner's end, their two plates were piled to precipitous heights, several inches beyond what one might call capacity. Both women were still hungry, but they had accomplished their goal—they showed respect to the level they felt warranted. And the ten-minute intense fight over who could grab and cover the bill hadn't even begun yet.

In her later years, Mrs. Lui continued to be sweet, kind, and gracious. Beneath this outwardly seemingly gentle veneer, however, was a strong brave woman. She was one of the few women in China to have a college degree in those days. Her toughness had been honed during the Japanese occupation of the late thirties. She had smuggled large sums of money in various currencies in the hollow part of her bicycle handlebars to help fund the Chinese underground. If caught, she would have been tortured and shot by day's end.

She also joined a resistance group and traveled to country sides with a theatre troupe during the Sino-Japanese war, putting on anti-Japanese propaganda plays in remote villages, another capital offense. She hinted to her children that she had been nearly caught on numerous occasions, but like so many parent-child communications, never elaborated on the details.

45.
SWIMMING TO A NEW LIFE

It was a moonless and totally dark night except for a few dim lights emanating from somewhere in the middle of Deep Bay, near Shenzhen, Mainland China sometime in 1972. Five minutes after the guard dogs had made their rounds, Hong Li and her friend slipped unobserved into the coastal waters. For several months they had prepared for this night by taking long distance swims off a remote beach further up the coast. Now gripped by both fear and adrenaline, they began their four-mile swim across the South China Sea towards Hong Kong—and towards freedom. They were fortunate to embark on a night blessed with good weather and calm seas, and had chosen an entry point along the beach that purportedly had the loosest security.

The only visual reference they had once in the water was a relatively bright beacon, midway across Deep Bay Channel. As they reached the beacon, they gained renewed strength and hope and shook off the energy-sapping cold that threatened their success. They had officially entered Hong Kong waters. Only two miles to go and no more fear of being intercepted by Communist patrol gunboats. They next made their way towards the newly visible lights of Shui Wai, known for the cultivation of large oyster beds. Even though the two were by now strong swimmers, the dimness of their guiding-lights, uncertain tides, and playing hide and seek with

Chinese gunboats patrolling those waters stretched what would normally be a journey of three hours into closer to six hours.

Even with lurking sharks added to the hazard list, three to four dozen swimmers (the unofficial count was probably several times higher,) successfully braved this crossing to Hong Kong each month in 1972; it was unknown how many failed in their attempts.

Finally reaching land, as coached by their enablers from the Mainland and previous successful refugees, the pair reported to the first Hong Kong police station they could find. The word was out that they were at little risk of being sent back to the Mainland. Hong Li's father had instructed her to contact Mr. Lui, a longtime pre-revolution friend, for his assistance once they arrived. He made her memorize Mr. Lui's phone number before he tearfully bade her goodbye.

Hong Li followed her father's instructions and called Mr. Lui from a payphone as soon as she could. Mr. Lui immediately arranged to have her picked up and brought to their home in Repulse Bay. True to her father's expectations, he helped her get settled as best he could, once she recovered from the arduous ordeal of her escape.

Hong Li was ill equipped to live on her own when she first arrived, so the family hired her as a live-in companion for their youngest daughter, who suffered from a developmental disability. During the next couple of years, they treated her like a daughter and helped her adjust to the culture shock of Hong Kong, learn rudimentary English, and accumulate modest savings.

In the meantime, Hong Li was delighted when her brother, Hong Xian, who had escaped to Hong Kong a few years earlier, was able to make contact with her. Thereafter he often visited the Luis' home and was treated as family as well, often meeting her for lunch at Mr. Lui's office.

Mr. Lui knew Hong Li would eventually need to integrate with Hong Kong society and suggested: "Hong Li, I have many friends in the restaurant business here in Hong Kong. They are desperate to find trained chefs to meet the growing demands of their business. With your talent, I can easily get you into a chef training program that would lead you to a successful career and give you a chance to improve your English as well."

"Thank you so much, Uncle. I appreciate your offer, especially as you have done so much for me already. But I am afraid to remain in Hong Kong, as its sovereignty is so uncertain. They say that if Mainland China takes over Hong Kong, refugees such as myself will be treated as traitors and we would be executed. I must leave here. To be safe, I must get as far away from China as possible." (The transfer of Hong Kong's sovereignty from the United Kingdom to China, known as the "Handover", did take place July 1, 1997.)

The Luis switched strategies from searching for a Hong Kong solution to her future to searching for an out-of-country marriage solution.

46.

THE ALMOST ROBBERY

–

OFFICE INSECURITY

After Mr. Lui left the Shanghai Commercial Bank in the 1930s where he had worked with Enlin Pan, Sr., he began his career as an entrepreneur, starting with the purchase of a small candy factory. Enlin's prediction proved correct: Mr. Lui had been a so-so banker but became a brilliant businessman.

Forty years later in the 1970s, Mr. Lui managed all his business interests from a small suite of offices in Hong Kong's Central District with the support of seven employees.

Mr. Lui was paranoid about being robbed so like other office occupants in his building, he installed a double layer of security:

1. To minimize visitors, he conducted most of his face-to-face business activities at locations other than his office suite. Those few visitors who did need to be on the premises were given a special doorbell ring code to gain access.

2. He had a small alarm bell installed under his senior assistant's desk in the outer offices and another bell installed under his own desk in his inner office. Pressing either bell would directly alert building security guards who then, in turn, were to contact the police.

The Event

It was the slow time of day during lunch break, and as it was Mr. Lui's routine to lunch late, he was on the phone in his inner office addressing a tense and difficult family matter. His office during that time of day was down to minimum staffing of three employees; the other four would not return from lunch for another half hour.

The special access code announced that a known associate wished to gain access at the door. A clerk automatically responded to the code and buzzed in whomever was there.

The door flung open; three young, masked assailants rushed in brandishing large knives, shouting "Everyone on the floor! Hands over your head! No talking!" A fourth conspirator remained in the hall as lookout.

While one of the thugs kept a watchful eye on the three employees holding them at bay with a switchblade, the remaining two barged into Mr. Lui's inner office.

To intimidate Mr. Lui into quick submission, the lead thug placed his knife against Mr. Lui's throat and shouted, "Open the safe, old man, or I'll slit your throat!"

SLAM! Mr. Lui brought his right hand down onto the desk with enough force to startle even himself. He was mad and showed it. He pulled the phone slightly off his ear and shouted, "Put that thing down! Can't you see I'm on an important call? Your robbery will just have to wait! This is important." Then, he returned the phone back to his ear and ignored the would-be thieves.

The diversion was just long enough for the assistant to surreptitiously push his alarm button, alerting building security, and then resume his meek hostage posture.

The lead thief, stunned by Mr. Lui's unexpected response, lowered his knife. "*This was not to plan,*" he thought, *This man was supposed to grovel and beg for his life, not shout at me. Oh my god, he's just as bad as my father.* Both thieves just stood there dumbfounded trying to figure out their next move. Finally, the lead recovered his composure and tried to retake control. He resumed his more assertive posture of Plan A. But before he could say anything, Mr. Lui took over once again by raising the palm of his hand towards him, blocking eye contact, and continued his call.

The two thieves stared at each other, hoping the other knew what to do.

Finally Mr. Lui hung up, turned towards the robbers and spoke to, or rather lectured them. "You two are such idiots—you don't even know how to rob someone properly. What you two are trying to do is like blowing up an empty, unlocked safe. We don't keep money here. No one in this building does. The only things we keep in the safe are important documents and deeds—things we need to protect against fire or water damage. Any money involved is in the banks—that's what banks are for, you idiots!

"Here! Here's eight hundred and fifty dollars—that's all I have on me. Do you really want to go to jail for eight hundred and fifty dollars? Now get out of here before you make things any worse for yourselves."

Their indecision was interrupted by their lookout rushing in from the hall screaming, "They're coming up the stairs. We gotta get out of here fast!"

Later, when Mr. Lui was asked by the police if he could identify any of the robbers, he replied, "Certainly. It was Hong Xian's friend. Hong Xian's the brother of our ward, Hong Li."

"How can you be so sure it was him?"

"I recognized his accent. It's the same as Hong Xian's and is very distinctive. Also, his friend forgot to remove his easily recognized ring with two golden dragons on the second finger of his left hand. Hong Xian has a matching one. They've been to my office before and are familiar with the layout here including the location of our safe, our staffing routine during lunch, and our office access procedure. I understand he's been out of work for the last couple of months, so he must be desperate for money."

The would-be-robbers were in custody by nightfall.

Even though Mr. Lui acted brazenly, he was quite shaken by the whole event, but seemed fully recovered after a few days had passed. The topic discussed among his children was: "If he had not been so angry, would he have acted so boldly? Was he that brave or just pissed?" They all agreed you don't want Mr. Lui pissed when he is your adversary.

When Hong Li learned it was her brother's friend who attempted to rob her benefactor, and her brother was involved, she burst into tears and offered to move out immediately. She was so humiliated that she never forgave him.

Mr. Lui told her she was not to blame and beseeched her to stay, but at the same time, at her request, renewed his search with a local marriage broker to find her a suitable husband—preferably one out of the country. She was a beautiful young woman and after living in the Luis' household for two years, had become far more sophisticated than when she escaped from the Mainland. With such credentials, the Luis were optimistic that a good match could be found.

After a few months' search, Hong Li narrowed her prospects down to two candidates. She consulted the Pans, who were familiar with life in America and were still living in Hong Kong at the time, about which of the two matches she should accept. One was a very wealthy young man from a prominent local family who was mentally challenged but whose union promised her a secure financial future—basically in exchange for caretaking. The second was a Hong Kong emigrant to the U.S.—Freddy, a butcher who owned a small business fifty miles south of San Francisco. He was a hard-working kind man who had returned to Hong Kong in hopes of finding a wife to start a family.

Shortly thereafter, on the Pans' advice, she married the butcher and joined him in California where she could begin her new life. Forty years later, she is happy and the proud mother of two successful sons.

47.
WE MUST HAVE LUNCH

"Phil!" Meimei yelled out to her business associate as she approached him in the hall at work. "I just heard. You're going to Hong Kong on a project next week. Is that true?"

"Yeah, for a week. I leave Monday."

"Wow, how exciting. You must look up my Uncle Lui. He's not my real uncle, but our families have been so close for so many years that I call him Uncle—in the Chinese sense that is. He would be so pleased to meet you. Just let him know you're my friend, and I'm sure he will make time for you. He knows all the ins and outs of Hong Kong including the top movers and shakers. He would be a great contact for you."

(Meimei always tried to send interesting people to Mr. Lui, knowing he delighted in meeting new people. One friend, the president of a construction company, presented him with a mounted piece of the Golden Gate Bridge cable salvaged from a cable refurbishing project. It was Mr. Lui's favorite gift—a conversation piece that was hard to beat.)

Ten days later, Phil completed his Hong Kong objectives ahead of schedule and had a few days to spare when he remembered, *Meimei asked me to give her uncle a call. You know,* he thought, *It might be kind of fun to see him. And she may be right, I might benefit from talking to someone with the inside scoop on what's happening here.* He picked up the phone in his room and gave Mr. Lui a call.

"Wei?"

"Ah, yes, is Mr. Lui there please?"

"Yes, this is he. Who is calling please?"

"Mr. Lui, my name is Dr. Phil Michaels from SRI in Menlo Park. I'm a close friend of Meimei's and…"

"Oh, you're Meimei's friend! How wonderful of you to call!"

"Yes. A good friend, actually. We've worked on several projects together. I'm in Hong Kong on some SRI related business. Meimei suggested that while here, I give you a call so…"

"You're Meimei's friend! Please, please, we must have lunch. When are you free?"

"Actually, that's what I was calling about. I'm mostly free for the next two days and…"

"I would so much like to meet you. Sooner the better. Would today at 12:30 work for you?"

"Why—yes, (long pause). I don't have any appointments until late this afternoon, so 12:30 would be ideal."

"Wonderful. Where, if I may ask, are you staying?"

"I'm staying at the Hotel Furama in Yau Tsim Mong. It's a little hard to find. Perhaps I should give you directions to find the place."

"Hotel Furama. No, that's okay. I think I know where it is. Yes, I'm quite sure. That's the thirty-two story hotel in Central District, isn't it?"

"Correct. Meet you at 12:30 then, in the lobby?"

"Yes, I'll be there at 12:30."

Phil wasn't sure what to expect or even how he would recognize Mr. Lui. Meimei did say he was in his mid-sixties, shorter than average, with thinning hair and always sported a giant smile that couldn't be missed.

Mr. Lui appeared right on time and immediately headed to meet Phil from across the lobby. Spotting Mr. Lui in a wrinkled, rather poorly fitting suit and sneakers, Phil's first thoughts were: *He doesn't seem that well-off. I think Meimei exaggerated his importance. Looks like he tried to dress up for me as best he could to make a good impression for Meimei's sake. And important people aren't usually so free for lunch. I'm going to get stuck with the lunch tab—oh well, he's Meimei's uncle, so I guess I don't mind. And besides, I should be able to expense it as a business meeting anyway.*

Mr. Lui began to greet Phil a good ten feet away before he was even able to grasp his outstretched hand accompanied by his giant signature smile, just as Meimei had foretold. He effused, "Dr. Michaels, it's so nice to meet you. Any friend of Meimei's is always welcome. Before we chat, where would you care to have lunch?"

Phil answered hopefully, "This coffee shop has a nice lunch. I ate here two days ago, and it was surprisingly good."

"Yes, but I hear they have an excellent buffet in the revolving restaurant on the top floor," Mr. Lui countered. "It has a very good reputation and great view. All the Hong Kong critics give it their top ratings. I think we should give it a try. After all, you should experience the best Hong Kong has to offer while you are here if you wish to understand how Hong Kong works."

Phil, picturing dollars flying from his pocket big-time, tried to persuade Mr. Lui that the coffee shop would be just fine while Mr. Lui maneuvered him towards the revolving restaurant's direct access elevator. Suddenly Mr. Lui seemed to lose his ability to comprehend English, a skill that abandoned him right up until the elevator closed behind them. Phil, fighting his tendency to go cheap, finally acquiesced and accepted his fate. Mr. Lui, as usual, prevailed.

When the elevator door opened at the top floor, Phil was impressed with the extensive buffet spread greeting them. He decided to enjoy himself and, what the heck, make the best of it.

Phil gorged on the wide variety of delicacies before him. It was not until halfway through the meal that he noticed Mr. Lui limited his consumption to a modest bowl of chicken and cabbage broth.

Maybe this lunch won't set me back so much after all, he mused.

Meanwhile, Mr. Lui was taking the opportunity to ask Phil numerous questions about his work, ambitions, and philosophy on life in general. Totally full of himself, Phil had a wonderful time chatting away, embellishing his self-directed responses, while Mr. Lui put into practice one of his most valuable people skills, that of a good listener.

Towards the end of the meal, somewhere between Phil's second and third dessert, Mr. Lui began to bend the contents of the conversation toward topics closer to home.

"Tell me, Dr. Michaels, are you enjoying your stay here in Hong Kong? And what do you think of Hotel Furama?"

"I find Hong Kong fascinating. I'd love to live here for a year to learn more about Chinese culture. And the hotel? It's quite good. In fact, better than most I've stayed at in Hong Kong—except perhaps, for a few minor details. But then I've only been here five days so far."

"Interesting. Just what are these minor details? I'd love to hear about them."

By now, Phil was used to Mr. Lui piling question upon question, so he didn't notice the shift in the inquiry's focus to the hotel.

After Phil finished his critique, Mr. Lui sat quite still for a moment, thinking.

"Dr. Michaels."

"Yes, Mr. Lui?"

"I would consider it a great honor if you would do me a personal favor."

"Of course. Happy to." Phil had, by this time, been so charmed by Mr. Lui that he would do almost anything for him.

"Would you mind repeating your most insightful critique of your stay in this hotel to a friend of mine? He just happens to be nearby."

"Why no, not at all," Phil responded, a bit confused, and sensing that, in all his talking and minimal listening, he might have missed something.

Mr. Lui raised his hand and made an almost imperceptible gesture with his index finger. Within seconds a tuxedoed man, erect with perfect posture, presented himself, "Yes, sir?"

"This is Dr. Phil Michaels, an expert business consultant from San Francisco who has a few comments he has graciously consented to share with us about this hotel. Please take notes."

The man bowed slightly, retrieved a notepad, and turned to Phil with a "Yes, sir?"

Phil, who still did not fully comprehend the scenario, repeated his monologue describing the shortcomings of the hotel and particularly of his room, while the man furiously scribbled it all down. When he finished, the man thanked him profusely, bowed slightly once again to Mr. Lui, and vanished.

Phil knew he had been had, but did not fully understand either how or to what extent. He did however, notice the tuxedoed man was not introduced by name. Finally, he asked Mr. Lui the critical question, "Who, may I ask, was that gentleman?"

The famous ear-to-ear smile Mr. Lui had been suppressing all though lunch broke its bonds as he gleefully responded, "Oh, him? He's my Manager."

Needless to say, no bill appeared for Phil's lunch, but a bottle of very high-end champagne did show up in his room that evening.

48.
NO WORDS NEEDED

The flight attendant reset the call button as she leaned in closer to the passenger to hear his request.

"Miss? Including our baby here, there are four of us scrunched into these three seats. It's pretty tight. By any chance, are any vacant seats available that one of us could move to give my family a bit more breathing room?"

"I'm sorry sir, this flight is completely sold out."

In a slightly more agitated voice, the passenger continued, "But Miss, that guy sleeping over there three rows up. He's taking up an entire row of three seats all by himself. That can't be right!"

"Oh, I see what you mean. You're crammed into one row—and he's got a row all to himself."

"Could you please speak to him? I don't want any trouble, but it doesn't seem fair that he should be allowed to grab the whole row on a sixteen-hour flight before anyone else could even get a chance to occupy at least one of those extra seats."

"I'll see what I can do."

Temporarily appeased, the man settled back into his seat with a less than convincing, "Thank you, I appreciate your taking care of this for us."

The flight attendant moved up the aisle to Mr. Lui's row where he was stretched out across three seats, apparently asleep.

She shook him gently.

"Sir, Sir, Sir! I'm sorry to disturb you but you cannot take up three seats on this plane. Others need the room and…"

At first Mr. Lui pretended he didn't speak English and muttered something in Chinese without opening his eyes—a favorite trick of his when he wanted to be mischievous.

"Sir! Sir! I am sorry, but you cannot take up three seats on this flight."

Mr. Lui opened one eye, smiled, pulled his hand out from under his blanket, and without even looking at the flight attendant, held up three adjacent seat tickets long enough for her to fully understand the situation.

"Three tickets—three seats—all under one name—oh—I see—no problem. Oh. Oh! Excuse me sir! I'm sorry to have disturbed you. I did not understand. I will not bother you again."

She returned to the complaining passenger to explain, "Sir, the passenger occupying that row of seats paid for all three seats so they are his to use as he wishes. Officially, those seats are taken."

"Oh," responded the put-out passenger, completely caught off guard by her explanation. As she left, he muttered under his breath, "Still doesn't seem fair somehow."

Mr. Lui was recovering from an invasive surgery conducted in northern California and was just complying with his doctor's recommendation, "You must avoid remaining in a seated position for any extended length of time. So I recommend you postpone your return to Hong Kong for, at a minimum, two more weeks."

Strictly following his doctor's recommendation would prevent his timely return, and even a first-class seat would keep him in a partly seated position. Mr. Lui solved this problem by purchasing three adjacent seats in economy class. As he was quite short, the total width of three economy seats enabled him to lay flat across the seats. Ironically at that time, purchasing three economy tickets from San Francisco to Hong Kong was not much more expensive than buying one first-class ticket anyway.

49.
HEAD HOUSEKEEPER

Ah Hing had been with the Lui family for what seemed like forever. She joined them shortly after World War II when she was a teenager and gradually morphed into more of a family member than head housekeeper. She was the only member of the household staff who dared to contradict Mrs. Lui when she was wrong.

Mr. Lui advised several of their staff on how to save a portion of their wages and invest wisely for their future—some heeded his advice but of course, most didn't. Ah Hing was wise enough to observe Mr. Lui's financial aplomb, so she followed his advice to the letter. Accordingly, when she reached her early sixties, she was able to retire. She paid cash for a couple of modest condos in Hong Kong which she rented out and could retire quite comfortably on the income she received…quite rare for one who had been in domestic service her entire working life.

Ah Hing decided to retire, but not in Hong Kong. She had, for the past few years, harbored a strong yearning to return to her village on the Mainland where she had fond memories of a happy childhood. Her remaining years could be a simple, peaceful life surrounded by family members and old friends still in the vicinity. She fantasized about long afternoons sipping tea while reminiscing with her few remaining long-term friends. The Luis tried to persuade her to remain in Hong Kong, given the still unstable financial and political conditions on the Mainland and did not trust the motives of the villagers attempting to lure this millionaire (compared to them) back to their fold.

"You don't know what's really going on in your village! The Chinese government can change the rules on a whim with no notice. They have no love for outsiders, even those who grew up in China. They consider anyone who fled to Hong Kong a traitor. You have no security, nothing to protect you. They are still corrupt even though they claim to be law abiding. I implore you. Stay! Your life will be so much better here, and you will be safe!"

"My family has assured me things have changed for the better over these past few years. They are very excited for me to return and be part of the family again. They've arranged for me to buy a small house with two bedrooms at a very reasonable price."

Ah Hing would not relent to the Luis' urging, so they acquiesced and wished her well. Mr. Lui did prevail in one aspect of her arrangements, however.

"At least let me manage the bulk of your savings here in Hong Kong for the next few years until you're convinced they are not just after your money. They have a different reality than you and consider you super rich by their standards."

"I'm sure that's not the case, but my money will be safer with you managing it for me, and anyway, it has a better chance of holding its value here in Hong Kong than on the Mainland."

The first few letters following her settling into her new house seemed to confirm her expectations. She wrote about how happy she was and how delightful she found the little house in her small village. She asked that additional funds be sent to her and, as these amounts were relatively modest, Mr. Lui complied.

Months later the tone of her letters changed, and the amounts requested rose dramatically. Mr. Lui became alarmed and made up excuses as to why larger amounts were not feasible.

Mr. Lui used his Mainland contacts to investigate Ah Hing's actual living conditions and situation, only to discover that she was ill and being held a virtual prisoner in her own home. Her so-called friends and relatives forced her to write letters requesting ever-increasing amounts of money. She did not have access to good medical care, and the Luis feared for her wellbeing.

Mr. Lui knew the longer he waited to act, the more difficult it would be to assist her, so he formulated a plan—a bold plan that included numerous bribes and his usual brand of audacity.

The ambulance attracted considerable attention, as such a shiny modern vehicle had never before been seen in this remote village. It came to an abrupt stop at the front door of Ah Hing's home where she was being held. Several very important looking people jumped out. A doctor and two medical assistants, all in white coats, rushed into the house and announced that Ah Hing had had a serious heart attack. Meanwhile, outside the house, two very officious uniformed soldiers kept onlookers at bay.

Ah Hing had no idea what was happening and almost did have a heart attack on the spot just seeing all the people rushing into her room. They calmed her down as best they could, and then the "doctor" bent over and whispered into her ear, "Mr. Lui has arranged everything. Please pretend you are having a heart attack."

Mr. Lui's name had a magical effect on Ah Hing. She immediately grasped the situation, and began to feign, as best she could muster, someone having a heart attack.

Within twelve minutes of their arrival, they were speeding out of town, long before the greedy, conniving relatives figured out they had been duped. Within six hours, the ambulance drove back over the border into the Northern Territories, then made its way into Hong Kong proper on Victoria Island. An hour later, a weeping and most grateful Ah Hing was resting in the Luis' home in Repulse Bay—where she belonged. She never left Hong Kong after that and absolutely refused wages, expressing joy at just being reunited with her real family.

50.
GARDENER

In 1954, Mr. Lui purchased a piece of land in Repulse Bay on which two years later, he hired an architect to build a state-of-the-art house as a 'weekend retreat'. He fell in love with the scenery and peacefulness of the large house, and moved his family with 7 children there permanently from Happy Valley in 1958-59. During this era, the Hong Kong government decided to ease overcrowding in Hong Kong Central by expanding housing in the relatively undeveloped Repulse Bay. To this end, the government held lotteries for people who wished to acquire leases on newly platted lots. The Luis acquired one such lease as a backyard.

(The Hong Kong government officially owns all property in Hong Kong while "resident-owners" hold long-term renewable leases permitting them to build on and occupy these properties. Properties built before 1984 have guaranteed renewal clauses in their leases; those built between 1984 and 1997 may or may not have renewal clauses in their leases, and those built after 1997 mostly have their leases expiring in 2047.)

"Not a great investment, HM. You got the rights to a lot at the very top of the hill," sympathized his friends. "There is no way you could gain access to your property, much less build a driveway to it—it's much too expensive. Can't be done."

"But this lot is so much larger than lots farther down the hill—it more than compensates for what you call its *inferior location* but what I call an opportunity. And think of the view. Plus the parcel is bigger than a football field—huge by Hong Kong standards, and I got it at a cut rate price!" Many years later it proved to be one of the most valuable lots in all of Hong Kong, with a USD value in the mid eight figures.

Mr. Lui and his adjacent downhill neighbors agreed to share in the cost of building a driveway through all the mutual properties up to his lot, with the property owners towards the top of the hill paying a proportionately larger share of the costs. Then he enlisted a man named Ah Gong in 1952 to excavate his final driveway extension by hand. Ah Gong jumped at the chance to take on this job, estimating it would take at least two years to complete. He was grateful for any long-term employment where he could work alone, as he was an ex-con who had just been released from jail. He served time for his part in a high-profile robbery and hoped to stay out of the limelight while distancing himself from his former underworld connections.

Two years later, in 1954, the driveway and construction of the house were complete. Ah Gong stayed on as the Luis' landscaper and gardener. His fierce looks, reputation, and assumed mob connections made their home exceedingly secure. As a final security coup d'état, the Luis' dozen guard dogs had free-run of the grounds.

As the family grew to seven children, they decided to make their Repulse Bay home their permanent residence.

Despite all their security, a twenty-three foot python (as reported in the local newspaper,) managed to find its way onto their grounds late one afternoon and stirred up quite a ruckus with the dogs. By the time Ah Gong located the python, it was in the middle of swallowing whole, a six-month old puppy. Ah Gong managed to pull the puppy from the python's stomach but not before it had been suffocated by the snake's constrictions.

As a souvenir of the event, Mr. Lui proudly displayed a photo of the python wrapped several times around Ah Gong's body taken by the press (they got there first) while they all waited for wildlife protection representatives to show up. Ah Gong explained he was used to handling large snakes and felt in little danger of being seriously hurt.

The family suspected, however, that the presence of this photo over Mr. Lui's desk of Ah Gong being embraced by the giant python provided little reassurance to applicants being interviewed for domestic staff positions.

Ah Gong would often find small to medium snakes on the grounds. When he did, the seven Lui children were fascinated to watch him carry a freshly caught snake into the auxiliary kitchen, suspend it live by its tail, slit it lengthwise, remove what were considered by traditional Chinese medicine to be health-promoting organs, and pop them into his mouth raw. "Good for long life," he would proclaim to the kids with a wide bloody grin.

One morning they noticed he had lost a tooth. "Ah Gong," they advised, "Your tooth is broken! You need to see a dentist."

"No need. Happens all the time. Dentist, too expensive. Super Glue works just fine. Good as new."

Ah Gong was impressed by Mr. Lui's skill in investing, and he followed his guidance just as Ah Hing, the housekeeper, had. Like her, he was able to accumulate a tidy sum after twenty-five years religiously following Mr. Lui's investment advice.

One day he approached Mr. Lui:

"Mr. Lui. My friend tells me XYZ stock is a very good buy and about to announce spectacular earnings. He says we both can become very rich if we buy now. Do you think I should buy?"

"No. It is a very bad company, run by crooks. Avoid."

Next day. "My friend swears you are wrong and tells me I'm missing a chance of a lifetime, so I'm investing half of everything I have into this stock."

"Do as you wish, but I advise against it."

Ah Gong lost big on his ill-advised investment three months later when the company declared bankruptcy, and its officers were arrested for fraud. He learned his lesson and henceforth stuck to Mr. Lui's advice. His savings eventually recovered most of their value, thanks to Mr. Lui.

51.
WAIT! THERE'S MORE... SHORTS

Too Generous

Mr. Pan, a very compassionate boss, constantly worried about the welfare of his employees and their families. Many times, upon hearing that one of his employees was experiencing financial difficulties that a few hundred dollars would easily resolve, he would instruct his secretary, Miss Lee, to transfer funds from his special personal account (set up for this purpose) into his employee's account. This transfer would always be done anonymously, as Mr. Pan did not wish to draw attention to himself. An invisible angel.

One day, it happened. "Miss Lee, Mr. Zhou's wife, has just given birth to their fourth child—that makes two boys and two girls so far and he's only twenty-three. Could you please transfer $125 to his account from the special account? Babies are expensive."

"I'm sorry, Mr. Pan, but I cannot do that."

"Oh, Miss Lee? And why is that?"

"You gave away too much money already this month. You only have a balance of $15 remaining in that account."

Elevator Operator's Sick Wife (Hong Kong)

"You look terrible, Albert. Anything the matter?"

"No. It's nothing, Mr. Lui," Albert responded as he closed the elevator door. "Just a little hay fever."

"No, that's not it. You've been crying. I can see you're quite upset. Tell me. What's the matter?"

"It—it's my wife. She's quite ill and I can't afford a doctor and I…"

Mr. Lui went to his office and called the building manager. "Hello, this is Mr. Lui. Albert, the elevator operator will be out for the remainder of the day. See to it a replacement is sent over immediately. And make sure he is not docked pay for missing any work today. Do you understand?" (Nobody dared to disobey Mr. Lui's 'suggestions')

Then he returned to the elevator and waited until Albert's replacement arrived.

"Come with me, Albert."

"I can't. I'll lose my job!"

"Do not worry, it's all been arranged."

When they reached the building's front entrance, Mr. Lui's car was waiting with the motor running. "Albert, give the driver your address."

They picked up Albert's wife and proceeded to Mr. Lui's personal doctor's office where she was seen immediately. He waited with Albert for over four hours until the doctor assured them his wife was out of danger. As a final gesture of kindness, he covered all of Albert's wife's medical bills and deflected Albert's profuse thank you, thank you, thank you's.

Mr. Lui was a tough and successful businessman on the surface, but scratch that surface and you found a fair man; a man of compassion.

How Much?

Mr. Lui (or HM as he was most often referred to by friends and associates) was getting tired of petty thieves constantly pilfering his prestigious Mercedes hood ornament. He noticed that the lobby of the Hotel Miramar, of which he was a major owner, sported ashtrays decorated by three inch chrome "HM" initials of the same style and size as his hood ornament. He commissioned a craftsman to adapt the ashtray initials so they could be attached to the hood of his car. This made an impression on his friends, as he rarely shared how he accomplished this feat. His seven children, skeptical as is common among offspring, claimed his initials actually stood for "How Much?"

Sometimes, Discipline may be Necessary, but Pain is Not.

As the number of children in the Lui family grew and spanned a wide range of ages, the middle group coalesced into a preteen gang of four. The older two siblings busied themselves with their teenage interests, and the youngest toddler concentrated on what toddlers do. These emboldened middle four were the perpetrators of juvenile mischief in the household and were subject to subsequent discipline.

Placing dead flies in their tutor's black sesame broth and chalk dust in her almond broth were a few examples of their attempts at terrorizing the poor, underappreciated but somewhat mean tutor. (Not really. As adults they later became friends, and she lived to a ripe old age.)

If a mischievous act were particularly egregious, the mother/judge/jury/enforcer would have the maid assemble the offenders in the punishment room. There their mother would have them line up and apply as many and as firm caning strokes in turn to their bottoms as she thought appropriate.

The children would whimper in pain with the administration of each stroke, but once they exited, could not suppress a small hidden smile—for they shared a secret with their co-conspirators.

"Boy, Mama is really clueless," they agreed. "She never notices that the maid hides a thin unobtrusive book in our pants so the cane blows hardly hurt at all."

They formed a pact. "None of us shall ever tell," they agreed, "for if she found out, it would really hurt." They were rather proud of themselves in the belief that they had outfoxed their mother.

Years later, while visiting their family home and fondly reminiscing childhood experiences, they asked their mother's head maid,

"Did you know, Lee Chiang, the young maid we had for a few years, used to put books in our pants when mother was about to punish us?"

"Of course I did. I told her to."

"Wow, that was great, thank you. Do you think Mama ever suspected that we had books protecting us?"

"You four were so clueless." With that the head maid laughed. "Of course she did. After all, she was the one who told me to tell the maid to place them there in the first place!"

Money Was Short

After Enlin's job at the bank disappeared, following the Communist takeover of mainland China, the Pans found themselves in America with little income. At one point Emma was down to her last $50 and expected no additional income for a couple weeks. That's when she discovered, while hanging laundry on the building's rooftop clotheslines, that her neighbor's plight was even more serious than hers. The neighbor needed roughly that amount to take her youngest child to the doctor to treat a severe ailment and buy milk for her three kids. Emma was so touched she lent her neighbor her last $50, which never came back. Those were lean times—and those were good people.

Sometimes Long-term Planning Isn't So Long

To fulfill his duties as the President of the China Travel Service, Enlin was constantly on the go. In late 1942 he spent so much time in India that it was prudent for his employer to secure a full-time hotel suite to simplify his erratic housing requirements. It was an upscale 4-star hotel that provided him the services and space he required without being too ostentatious. One of the amenities was the ever-present personal hall boy stationed just outside his door. The hall boy's sole responsibility was to carry out any tasks a hotel guest might require—deliver messages, send for food, assure laundry was done in a timely manner, fetch items from the lobby, and track down specialists if so desired. At this time in India's history, unskilled labor was incredibly cheap, so hiring one hall boy per hotel suite was a relatively inexpensive amenity, while also providing entry-level local employment.

The hall boy's compensation was covered by the hotel plus any token tips from guests as they deemed appropriate. One day after several weeks of residence, Enlin felt particularly generous and slipped his hall boy a larger than normal tip. The hall boy was very excited about what was, to him, a windfall.

Then, for some unbeknownst reason, the hall boy vanished. On the third day of his disappearance, Enlin started to become alarmed. On morning four, just as Enlin was about to inquire at the desk as to what might have befallen his hall boy, he reappeared.

"Oh, thank goodness you're back. I was worried. I thought you were sick or had an accident. Are you okay?"

"Oh yes, *Sahib* I'm fine. Did you not get my message?"

"No, what message?"

"I asked my friend two doors down the hall to tell you I would not be coming to work for three days. He must have forgotten."

"Well thank heavens you're all right. Why were you gone? Was it a family problem? What kept you away for so long?"

"Oh no *sahib*. Nothing happened. I didn't come to work—didn't need to."

"Didn't need to?"

"Certainly, I didn't need to. I had enough money for three days, so why work?"

Future tips were smaller and more frequent.

Language Issues

A local banker found himself sitting next to a Chinese gentleman during a Cincinnati Chamber of Commerce-sponsored dinner. The banker was looking forward to hearing the guest speaker, a man who had been on the cover of *Newsweek* and was reputed to have considerable international currency expertise. The talk's topic was, "International Currency Controls, Good or Bad?"

The banker had never met a Chinese individual before and felt a bit awkward in his presence. He wanted to be friendly, but he could not figure out how to break the ice. Finally, when the second course was being served, he gestured to his Chinese companion, raised his spoon, and asked, "You like soupy?"

His Chinese companion smiled, held up his own spoon, and nodded to the affirmative. Then the master of ceremonies announced that night's speaker, at which point Enlin surprised the banker by standing up and moving to the dais. He gave his financial speech with numerous technical details in flawless English with no trace of an accent. (He had, after all, been an English professor in China many years before.) His speech was very well received. After he answered several questions from the floor, he returned to his seat next to the banker, raised his glass and asked, "You like speechy?"

They both laughed.

RELATIVE SPEAKING: MORE RESCUED STORIES

**1988
The Future:
Emma & Her Six Grandchildren**